Managing Differently™

Getting 100% from 100% of your people 100% of the time

James O. Rodgers, CMC
with
Maureen Hunter, Ph.D.

Oakhill Press
Winchester, VA

10 9 8 7 6 5 4 3 2 1

Book design and production by Bookwrights Design
Jacket design by Michael Komarck
Printed in the United States of America

Library of Congress Cataloging-in-Publication Data
on file with the Publisher

ISBN 1-886939-57-8

Oakhill Press
1647 Cedar Grove Road
Winchester, VA 22603
800-32-BOOKS

Dedication

This book is dedicated to my "other" mother, the late Lottie Dudley, and her alter ego, my wife and business partner, Sharon.

Contents

Preface

I learned early in my career as an executive that if you profess to know something well, you should be able to express it in a few words. Over the last five years I have developed and refined the principles and concepts in this book. It began as a collection of writings (thoughts, observations, essays, articles, course designs, and research notes) that totaled nearly *five hundred pages!* That was when I thought I knew a lot about this topic. However, the more I observed, tested, and learned about the ideas presented here, the shorter the manuscript became. When the book whittled down to around one hundred pages I thought, *Now's the time.* I hope you agree.

I wrote this book for you: the man or woman who faces the challenge of juggling the diverse requirements of your people with the results-focused requirements of your organization every day. I call this challenge the *100 percent imperative:* getting 100 percent from 100 percent of your people 100 percent of the time.

In this book I help you see why a focus on management skills and Managing Differently (especially at the first-line and middle levels) is so essential to realizing this potential. I discuss the fundamentals of Managing Differently including the core principles. I also discuss the application of the principles of Managing Differently to the four phases of the employee-manager relationship.

If you are looking for hard data to support this work you will be disappointed. Often my colleagues and I observe our clients caught in the data trap: when they finally start to explore diversity management and/or inclusion they expend enormous amounts of time and energy collecting data, comparing their results to other companies, and generally discussing the interpretation of the data. While the data has a role to play in an organization's diversity efforts, focusing on the data may be just an excuse to avoid taking action on things you already know need attention.

I prefer to focus on the human level, that is, what happens between two people—a manager and her direct report—as they strive to make themselves and the organization successful. This, after all, is at the heart of the hard data. Therefore, what I present in this book is based on my experiences and observations as well as the wisdom of my colleagues and clients. You too have developed the wisdom of experience when it comes to interacting with others. You know in your heart and your gut when you have connected with another person in a way that allows him to do his best. I am going to ask you to trust this as you learn about Managing Differently.

Finally, this is more of a why-to rather than a how-to book. I believe that if you learn and internalize a set of guiding principles and are equipped with simple tools, then you will make different and better choices in your managerial behavior. These choices will be appropriate for you and the people who work with you. This book presents a way of thinking about the challenge of Managing Differently so that you can expand your range of behavioral choices. You will find a model, a set of principles, and a couple of tools to help you. I have also included key learning points and reflection questions at the end of each chapter to help you think about the concepts in terms of your own experience and challenges.

Choosing to be the manager for your people and to get the best from each one is a courageous decision. This book will help you affirm that you are on the right track.

Acknowledgments

First I want to thank God for calling me and permitting me to do this "holy" work.

In addition, thousands of people contributed to this book. Most don't even realize it. They are the people I've worked with, advised, observed, facilitated learning for, and collaborated with over the past thirty years. They include the staff and faculty of J.O. Rodgers & Associates Management Consultants—the finest group of people in the universe.

I also would like to acknowledge several senior-level clients who have helped me get to this point. In particular, I thank:

Mike Warren, CEO of Energen & Alabama Gas Corporation, for ten years of friendship and encouragement (and occasionally following my advice).

David Ratcliffe, CEO of Georgia Power, for offering his own wisdom and experience as a CEO and change agent to help me refine and validate this work.

In addition, I would like to thank:

- Jack Ward, CEO of Russell Company
- R. Roosevelt Thomas, my friend and *the* thought leader for the field of Diversity Management
- Isaac Blythers, president of Atlanta Gas Light Company
- Frank McCloskey, vice president of diversity action at Georgia Power
- James Dallas, chief information officer of Georgia Pacific

- Alan Weiss, CMC[1] (the ultimate consultant)
- Carol Young, director of global diversity at Texaco-Chevron
- Roger Herman, CMC (author and futurist)
- Booker Rice, executive vice president–retired, The Prudential
- Booker Izell, vice president, The Atlanta Journal Constitution, a Cox Enterprises company

Lastly, I would like to thank Maureen Hunter, Ph.D. (Dr. Moe), for five years of loyalty, encouragement, prodding, and annoying rightness as we developed and tested these concepts, and Angel Reed of Virtual HQ for her creativity and patience in taking this project from manuscript to reality.

Introduction

Over the past fifteen years, I have observed how people respond as their organizations launched diversity initiatives. My associates and I have had conversations with tens of thousands of people as we facilitated diversity-related learning activities for small and large groups. By far, the most frequently asked question has been, "Has my manager been to this?" People say things like, "My manager is still doing the same thing," or "She needs to be here," or "He needs to come back for a refresher." Oftentimes, the question comes from managers who have managers. While many of these people acknowledge that some significant changes have occurred at the macro level with respect to diversity (leaders support it, policies reflect it, signs on the wall promote it, etc.), they are still dissatisfied with their daily experiences with their direct manager. Does this sound familiar to you? Could it possibly be directed at you?

Managing people is difficult. Diversity makes it all the more complex. No two employees are going to respond exactly the same to any idea, issue, mandate, or question. Each individual whom you support has her own set of talents, attitudes, opinions, needs, desires, expectations, and motivations. Yet, if you are like managers at many organizations, you are expected to manage employee diversity effectively and are being held accountable for doing so. Also, employees are watching to see if you are walking the talk. It's no wonder that many managers feel beleaguered under the circumstances. After years of exposure to diversity and management training—after being encouraged to take it seriously, challenged to understand its complexity, forced to comply with the program, and asked to demonstrate your new awareness—you still wonder, "What am I supposed to do?" *Managing Differently* is intended to take you to that next step in the process by providing principles and recommending behaviors that will help you get the best from all your employees.

My experience tells me that we need to focus our diversity efforts on managers. Over the past two decades organizations have focused on representation (affirmative action), interpersonal relationships (valuing/understanding differences), and creating cultures that leverage diversity for competitive advantage. While all of these layers are important, at the heart of an organization that is able to make its employees feel valued are managers who are able to engage those employees.

I have been involved with a number of companies (Texaco, Coca-Cola, and Georgia Power) who faced high-profile, expensive lawsuits involving employees. In each case it was not the policies, the senior leadership, the stated values, or the lack of commitment to equity and inclusion that created the discontent among employees. Instead, the plaintiffs' concerns could almost always be traced to ineffective managers who failed to listen and respond to them as members of the team.

During the employee lawsuit against The Coca-Cola Company in 2000, an article in a legal journal quoted one of the plaintiffs. His comment was so simple yet so profound. It expressed what, in my opinion, is at the core of every employee concern,

> There is a missing link in the discussion about diversity: the effective management of people. Similarly, the missing link in the discussion about management is diversity.

every employee decision to withhold effort, every disgruntled employee, every alienated team member, and yes, every employee lawsuit. When asked by the interviewer what he really hoped to achieve from the lawsuit, the employee said, "I just want[ed] to be heard."

Current research supports the importance of the manager-employee relationship. For example, research conducted by the Gallup Organization[2] suggests that effective managers focus on making sure all employees have the support, encouragement, and development they need to feel cared for, heard, and valued, and that their work matters.

Through observation and research, I have concluded that there is a missing link in the discussion about diversity: the effective management of people. Similarly, there is a missing link in the discussion about management, and that is diversity. The purpose of this book is to link the two.

Employees are diverse by the fact that they are human. So, what should you, as a manager, do day-by-day to effectively manage these employees? You should *manage differently*, which means learning to be an effective manager of people and then adapting to the unique needs of each individual while managing your own preferences, biases, stereotypes, and reactions (i.e., your diversity).

I would like to highlight three key phrases in this statement. The first key phrase is *manager of people*. Many organizations and managers place little value on solid people management skills. Therefore, people with the title "manager" are thoroughly

> Managing Differently is learning to be an effective manager of people and then adapting to the unique needs of each individual while managing your own preferences, biases, stereotypes, and reactions.

distracted from their core role. Instead of focusing on supporting other people and creating inclusive work environments, they are focused on the technical side of the business and doing other things that get attention and rewards.

The second key phrase is *adapting to the unique needs of each individual.* The effective diversity manager is flexible and adapts her style to get the best from each individual.

The last key phrase is *managing your own preferences, biases, stereotypes, and reactions.* The challenge of diversity is that it elicits reactions in each one of us based on our own backgrounds and experiences, that is, our own diversity. To be an effective diversity manager, you need to be more conscious of the ways that your own diversity influences your reactions to the people who report to you.

Oftentimes, a manager's first reaction when we begin to talk about Managing Differently is that her plate is already incredibly full and she can't handle another thing. You may have a similar reaction. My response is that I am only encouraging you to expand on what you already do. Here is a story that illustrates this point.

> *A farmer in South Georgia was plowing his field one day using an old John Deere tractor. For those who don't know, an old John Deere tractor has been a staple of farming in the rural South for decades. It features two small front wheels, oversized back wheels, a metal saddle seat, a long-stem steering wheel, and wide-open spaces for a cab.*
>
> *On this particular day, a John Deere salesman came along. Seeing the farmer sweating and dusty from a day of plowing, he stopped and said to the farmer, "Mr. Farmer, it sure is hot and dusty out today. I tell you what, you need a new tractor. You know, John Deere has a new line of field tractors that you wouldn't believe. They've got power steering, power brakes, AM/FM cassette stereo sound systems*

inside an air-conditioned enclosed cab with GPS, and a computerized crop tracking mechanism. I can see that you need one of our new tractors."

The farmer just looked at the salesman and said, "No sir, I don't need a new tractor. I'm not plowing as good as I know how with the one I got."

I heard this story from David M. Ratcliffe, CEO of Georgia Power. He used it to stress the importance of Managing Differently while opening a class called "Managing Differently" that all managers in his company were required to attend. His point and mine is this: Managing Differently is not an attempt to sell you a new tractor. As you know, every management consultant and guru with a new idea tries to position it as the next great thing that will save your company and make you a legendary leader. Managing Differently is not new or revolutionary. My hope is to provide a few new attachments to your old tractor or an updated users' guide to help you plow your field better using your old tractor. These new attachments are simply:

- A framework for understanding Managing Differently
- An understanding of the barriers that get in the way of Managing Differently
- A set of principles that guide your behavior
- A few tools to draw from as you manage others

The bottom line is that you have to manage people anyway, so why not optimize your efforts? The majority of the concepts contained in this book have been fashioned from over three decades of observing organizational life. I have been a technical contributor, technical manager, executive, and management consultant. I have done most of my work teetering between the hard-side (numbers, processes, strategies, and objectives) and the soft-side (human needs, perceptions, expectations, and motivations) of organizational life. From each of these unique positions, I have observed how employees, managers, and leaders respond to these daily challenges. I have come to recognize the absolute importance of people to the success of any enterprise. Given that all people are, by definition, diverse (that is, different from and similar to all other people), managing diversity is an ever-present challenge in every manager's life. I believe every manager has the capacity to rise to this challenge. Can you see yourself mastering this challenge?

What You Need to Know

1. Managing people is difficult.

2. Managing diversity is difficult.

3. Managing Differently is the missing link between effective people management and effective diversity management.

4. Managing Differently is learning to be an effective manager of people and then adapting to the unique needs of each individual while managing your own preferences, biases, stereotypes, and reactions.

5. You can master diversity and management. It only requires you to expand on what you already know and do.

Reflection

• Are you prepared to manage in the twenty-first century with increasing diversity as a fact of life?

PART ONE

❖ ❖ ❖

The Case
for Managing
Differently

CHAPTER ONE

As a Manager, Who Are You?

The practice of management, especially managing people, is, at best, a low-priority discipline for many of today's organizations. If this is the case in your organization, you may find the following with respect to your time and talent for managing people:

- There is relatively little premium (reward) for doing it well.
- There is more focus on operational results and the "technical" side of the business.
- You or other managers were promoted into managerial assignments because of your technical expertise.
- It's easier to just tell people what to do.
- You haven't had the training and coaching to fully develop your managerial skills.

Often I find that organizations do not communicate the importance of managing people. For example, when people tell me about their promotion to the managerial ranks, the conversation that takes place often sounds something like this:

Bob, we have really been impressed with your work. That solution you developed will probably become a standard for the industry. So, I wanted you to know how pleased we are to now have you join our management team. Congratulations!

Whether intended or not, the message in this pronounce-ment is: "Bob, you are good at what you do. Now, we want you to keep doing what you do while helping others learn to do it the way you do it." What is generally not said, of course, is the following:

> *By the way, Bob, this new position will require a totally different set of skills and abilities than you have demon-strated so far. None of the people you will support will do things exactly the way you do. You can expect a wide range of diverse needs, expectations, temperaments, preferences, and skills. Let me encourage you to study management, to learn what it involves and how excellent managers are able to balance all the complexity and competing interests of their unit. You will need to spend the vast majority of your time and effort developing unique ways to meet the needs of each unique personality you will be supporting. In addition, I know you love coding, but you will probably not get to do much coding in this position. You will have to watch and be supportive while other people do it differently.*

Without the words or the expectation in place, new managers are left to their own devices to figure out that managing is differ-ent from doing. For example, being an *engineering manager* should be different than being an *engineer*. A military commander must have different skills than the personnel he or she commands. A top-notch information technology manager should exhibit dif-ferent behaviors and habits than a top-notch programmer or sys-tems analyst. Being a customer service director should involve different behaviors than being a front-line customer service rep-resentative. What is the difference? Simply put, a manager's role is to get things done through others. As such, the bulk of a manager's time and the primary function for which they are accountable should be to support the people to whom they have been assigned. Support means making sure that those people have everything they need to do their jobs effectively. In other words, a manager's job is to create stars, not to be one.

With the need to do more with less, many new managers find that they have more than enough to do without taking time to learn effective management practices. If there is no corporate mandate requiring them to participate in a prescribed management training curriculum, many will not discover effective practices until years into their career and/or after a lot of trial and error. By then, many managers have become frustrated, anxious, overworked, bitter, or set in their ways. Unfortunately, many will tend to direct their bitterness toward the people they support. They start to say things like, "Why don't they do things the right way [translated, my way]?" "Why won't they leave their personal problems at home?" "What do they expect from me?"

Seasoned managers also have a number of reasons for not practicing effective management techniques. For example, although some managers are aware of the principles of management and know that managing is different from doing, they do not believe that they can or should practice the principles of management. They probably do not see any evidence that they need to change and adopt effective managerial behaviors. Even if they suspect that they should, they are not sure they can. After all, effective managerial behavior quite often requires them to do just the opposite of what their natural human tendencies would suggest.

Other managers do not believe they need to practice effective management because their managerial role models are not doing so. This is true even when the managers do not particularly like their managerial role model. The fact that their manager was able to survive as a manager without practicing effective management is a further indication of the low priority placed on good management skills.

Finally, many managers do not practice effective management because they feel they are doing okay without it. Instead, they continue to do the things that have earned them rewards in the past, mostly through their technical efforts. To practice management principles would make them uncomfortable, would violate their natural preferences, and would make them different from their peers.

Yet, effective management is a critical part of organizational success. Research has demonstrated that organizations that are able to engage and motivate their employees are more likely to outperform their peers in measures such as growth, revenue, stock price, and net income.[3] The companies identified by *Fortune* magazine as the best places for minorities and women to work outperform the Standard and Poor's 500. Therefore, even though the importance of managing people may not be recognized in your organization, you, as a manager, still serve a vital role.

Despite the popular notion that we need fewer managers and more leaders, I believe that *effective management is the defining element of effective organizations.* Management is not only about processes and technology; it is also about people. Its essential role is to create an environment that allows and promotes optimal levels of performance by individuals and teams. You might argue that not everyone is a top performer. In return, I ask why not? All people have strengths. All people have weaknesses. An effective manager identifies and uses all the talent available for the execution of the organization's goals and objectives. Peter Drucker has suggested that a manager has the task of making people's strengths effective and their weaknesses irrelevant.[4]

As a manager, you sit squarely in the critical path of your organization's ability to live out its mission, vision, and values, and to honor its culture. Senior executives make bold pronouncements about the kind of workplace they want to create. When the results don't match their words, they turn to you, the managers, and ask, "Why haven't you done it?" The people you support hear the bold pronouncements of the senior leaders and

> **Management is not only about processes and technology, but it is also about people.**

try to catch the vision. When they experience anything other than the perfection described by the leaders, they turn to you, the managers, and expect you to fix it. What a job!

> As a manager, you sit squarely in the critical path of your organization's ability to live out its mission, vision, and values, and to honor its culture.

What You Need to Know

1. Few organizations truly value and reward effective people management.
2. Managers are in the critical path of an organization's ability to realize its goals.
3. A manager's job is to create stars, not to be one.

Reflections

- Are you as good at managing people as you are at managing projects, budgets, technology, or time?
- Can you encourage, support, and develop people who do things differently than you?
- Can you balance the pronouncements of your leaders with the expectations of your employees?

CHAPTER TWO

Management and Diversity

When diversity first became an area of focus, many leaders would ask what managers needed to know and do differently. I would simply tell them to make sure their managers learned how to manage people effectively. That means learn and master behaviors that allow them to support people effectively, encourage people effectively, develop people effectively, give effective feedback, develop effective relationships, build effective teams, coach effectively, select the right people, and in the process, manage their own personal biases, preferences, and reactions effectively .

As you can imagine, such a simple prescription didn't gain much traction because everyone was looking for a magic pill, a silver bullet, a list of do's and don'ts. Well, fifteen years later, the answer hasn't changed.

When the term "Managing Diversity" was first introduced,[5] I immediately saw two distinct challenges contained in the concept. First, diversity. Diversity is challenging because it includes differences. People do not naturally appreciate, understand, or respect that which is different. The second is managing. Managing is challenging because few people agree on what it is or how to do it.

To some people, acting like a manager means being the boss. It requires them to have all the answers, to be right (even when they are not), and to call all the shots. To others, it means being the expert who shows everyone else how to do things the right way. Still others view the role as overseer, team leader, coach, facilitator, or support person. The manager's response to management interactions and their selection of managerial behavior is often a direct result of how they view the role of manager. As a result, many people began approaching managing diversity as a macro issue: how companies, leaders, and societies collectively respond to diversity. Little, if any, guidance was developed to help individual managers adapt to the increasing diversity that is a reality of work life. In addition, senior leaders of organizations began holding managers accountable for doing something (i.e. managing diversity) that they had not equipped the managers to do (and usually did not practice themselves).

I found myself thinking and talking in terms of "managing differently"[6] rather than managing diversity because I wanted to place the emphasis on management. For me, the important thing was, is, and will be the ability to manage everyone within your sphere of influence effectively—recognizing their diversity and yours. To fully understand what this means, you must be clear on what diversity is and what it isn't.

Defining Terms

1. Diversity is a fact of life—a new reality that affects business strategy.

Diversity is a word of many meanings that elicits a variety of reactions. By "diversity," I mean the mixture of human characteristics present in any group of people. These characteristics represent both differences and commonalities. Diversity has always been with us. Any two or more people, even identical twins, have some discernible differences as well as some obvious commonalities.

Diversity includes everyone; it is not only defined by race or gender. It extends to age, personal and corporate background, education, personality, career and community status, lifestyle, geographic origin, organization tenure, exempt/nonexempt status, and management/nonmanagement roles.

Dr. Roosevelt Thomas once made the point that diversity does not produce harmony or unity in an organization. In fact, you can expect just the opposite. However, harmony, by its very nature, requires diversity. *You cannot get four-part harmony by playing the same note four times.*

In many organizations (and in many people's mental models) the word "diversity" is used or thought of interchangeably with "race" and "gender." Therefore, when an organization begins to focus on diversity, it is not unusual for white managers to be told how they need to be more sensitive to minorities and women. At the same time, minorities and women (employees and managers alike) are hoping that the experience will help their white (particularly male) counterparts see the error of their ways. The need for this type of awareness to take place may exist, but for me there is an even broader need.

2. Diversity Management is a deliberate effort to manage the reality that diversity exists because we are human.

Every manager needs to have the ability to manage a diverse group of employees. This means that African American, Hispanic, or female managers are not automatically better at getting the best from their people because of their race, ethnicity, or gender. So, let me say it again. *Every* manager is on the hook for getting the best from his employees who, by virtue of the fact that they are human, are automatically diverse. Here's an experience that helped drive this point home for me.

In the early 1980s, I was transferred within AT&T from a management position in Birmingham, Alabama, to a high-profile position in New York City. I was already recognized as a pretty good manager of people, though not too keen on attention to technical details. In New York, I was given responsibility for developing the procedures for the new FCC access charges that were to take effect the following year. Naturally, I needed a team of technical specialists to complete this task. I'm from the South, so the only real differences I was familiar with were those between white people and black people. Even so, I felt that I knew what diversity "looked" like and was prepared to deal with anything. My team was like none I had ever experienced. It included a Jewish woman from Manhattan, an Irish man from Boston, a young (openly) gay male from Manhattan, a Portuguese woman from upper Massachusetts, a young Afro-Caribbean woman, an Italian American male from Brooklyn, a black male from Newark, New Jersey, and a guy from Iowa. (I didn't even know they grew people in Iowa.) Needless to say, this range of differences posed some management challenges for me.

For example, my only exposure to someone like John, the Italian American man from Brooklyn, was from the TV show Welcome Back Kotter. *That show had a character named Vinnie Barbarino (played by John Travolta) who was absolutely the funniest guy I had ever seen. I frequently found myself amused at John's accent and mannerisms. This was even apparent in team meetings when I would chuckle when John provided comments. Of course, that behavior caused John some concern. Luckily, John and I had a good enough relationship that he felt comfortable coming to me with his concerns. He told me that when I laughed at his remarks it made him feel that I did not appreciate what he had to offer the team. Of course, this was not my intent, but I was thankful that John pointed out my error. I was able to step back and realize the reason for my amusement (Vinnie Barbarino) and then adapt my style to recognize the serious contributions that John was making to the team.*

3. **Managing Differently is a set of principles and recommended behaviors to facilitate that effort.**

Diversity contributes to the complexity of the workplace. Imagine that you are juggling three balls and have become quite skilled at it over time. You are comfortable with the task and, in fact, have evolved to the point that the three balls you are juggling are your favorite (preferred) balls. Now imagine that the organization asks you to increase the number of balls to five. Your task immediately becomes more complex. You need greater hand speed and more coordination, and then your organization asks and requires that you juggle five objects of different size, shape, and weight. The complexity is magnified greatly. You not only have to manage with speed and coordination, but you also have to adapt to the varying requirements and expectations of the different objects. You have to manage differently than you had in the prior situation.[7]

How well you do this depends on how well you handle complexity. If all these adaptations are beyond your complexity capacity, you become frustrated and may experience some failure. If the condition persists, you may begin to dislike your responsibilities, and especially to resent the objects that are so different from the "balls" you had become comfortable with. You may think that the new objects are the cause of your current difficulty.

In today's world of work, complexity is the norm. We have increasing change, complex technology, skills obsolescence, more stakeholders to satisfy, mergers and acquisitions, new relationships, shifting expectations, larger spans of control, work teams, fickle customers, quality standards, downsizing, process reengineering, shortage of skilled workers, globalism, and an ever-changing list of government and regulatory concerns. *People did not create complexity, but they certainly add to it.* Complexity (including diversity) creates challenges for today's manager and often results in resentment toward those things (or persons) that contribute to stretching their capacity for complexity. Most of us prefer to avoid complexity, which often means avoiding diversity.

Added to that, corporate cultures have conditioned us to simplify our approach to management. This preference for simplicity sometimes causes managers to focus on quantitative data to the exclusion of people issues. After all, data is predictable, while people are not. We also tend to label managers as task-oriented or people-oriented, implying that no manager can be both. Managers who see no reason to complicate their lives with concerns for all aspects of management will, as a practical matter, make the decision to minimize complexity as much as possible. Simplification may seem reasonable, but it is a very dangerous decision. Constantly minimizing complexity hinders the development of your capacity to manage it.

The goal of Managing Differently is not to increase diversity (i.e., representation). The goal of Managing Differently is to increase the probability of getting world-class results, achieving business objectives, and thriving in an ever-changing world. This mix of differences and commonalities requires managers to adapt and rely on a range of managerial behaviors rather than a single dominant style.

In order to benefit from changes in the business environment, it is important to learn a new way of thinking about diversity, which includes understanding that diversity exists in all areas. Valuing a diverse workforce involves developing a positive environment for all employees. Managing Differently is the process of gaining a competitive advantage through your people. To accomplish this, you must buy into the principles of Managing Differently and take proactive steps toward living these principles.

Managing Differently enables an organization to tap, channel, and manage the potential that diversity represents. When managed effectively, diversity can be the source of creativity, innovation, commitment, and exceptional results. When ignored or mismanaged, diversity can be the source of contention, mistrust, divisiveness, and disillusionment. It can also be at the core of a sequence of events that escalates to litigation.

Isn't It Just Affirmative Action?

Because of the tendency to equate "diversity" with race and gender, many see an organization's diversity efforts as just another affirmative action program, which leads to a lot of confusion. Not many people really like the fact that we have to have an Affirmative Action policy. In a culture of rugged individualism, Affirmative Action seems inherently unfair. Why should anyone be given preference based on something they didn't earn, but were born with? The real issue is: why should anyone be "un-preferred" for something they can't change? On its face, the very idea is antithetical to the American way.

But let's look deeper. Affirmative Action has a negative impact on persons on both sides of the issue. To white men,[8] the only identifiable group not covered by the plan, it feels like blatant discrimination against them for being white and male. To members of protected groups who have real talent and ability, it feels like any accomplishment is tainted with the label ("she only got the position because they needed a woman"). So, a real argument can be made that Affirmative Action is not consistent with our values and should be eliminated.

So, why was it created in the first place? And why, as many will argue, must it continue to be in place? If we cut through all the noise (heated debate) and the legal definitions, the answer has to do with "trust."

After the Equal Employment Opportunity (EEO) laws were enacted, civil rights leaders pointed out that not much progress had been made in the early years. The laws were not having the expected impact. Based on this observation, many citizens did not trust the leaders of corporations and other institutions to change old patterns of hiring, promoting, and firing people. At their request, President Johnson created an executive order called

Affirmative Action to measure the progress toward equitable representation in institutions that were directly or indirectly connected to the government. Our federal officials knew how easily EEO laws could be circumvented or selectively enforced. So the government, as in most old-line American companies, knew that the way to enforce Affirmative Action was to establish a clear goal, put a measurement on it, and monitor it relentlessly. That's Affirmative Action in a nutshell.

People who argue for keeping Affirmative Action are basically suggesting that without it the old ways would come right back. In other words, they say, "We don't trust you to do the right thing." They are not necessarily suggesting any malicious intent, but since we are all so deeply conditioned to prefer people like ourselves, they are suspicious that decision makers would unconsciously revert to "old" practices.

Besides, as many will argue, something like Affirmative Action has always existed in our society. Some people—white men—have historically been favored or preferred based on something they didn't earn, while others (e.g., people of color and women) were excluded for something they couldn't change. Furthermore, the results of Affirmative Action have been noteworthy, but not spectacular. Those who have traditionally been in power (white men) still hold over 90 percent of the positions of power while representing less than half the population. The facts do not support that white men have been systematically excluded from consideration under Affirmative Action.

So, while Managing Differently is based on increasing trust, Affirmative Action is, and was always, built on distrust.

Managing Differently is not Affirmative Action. It's about every manager getting the best from his or her employees. This is the 100 percent imperative I spoke of earlier: *getting 100 percent from 100 percent of your people 100 percent of the time.*

What You Need to Know

1. Diversity is a fact of life.
2. Diversity Management is a deliberate effort to manage that reality.
3. Your behavior as a manager is influenced by your perception of the role of manager.
4. Managing Differently is a set of principles and tools to help you manage diversity effectively.
5. Affirmative Action was designed to measure progress toward equitable representation in organizations that are government, quasi-government, or a supplier to government.

Reflection

- Are you being held accountable for managing the diversity in your organization? If so, how?
- Are you equipped to do it?
- Do you think of Diversity Management as the same as Affirmative Action?
- Do you always try to minimize complexity in your work life? Does that include minimizing diversity?

Managing Differently: What's in It for You?

L et's face it. Your job as a manager is already pretty tough. You may feel caught in the middle between higher-ups and employees who have unrealistic expectations of you. So if we had the opportunity to talk face-to-face, you would probably tell me you have enough to think about without worrying about Managing Differently. My response to you is that even with all of the stuff on your plate, you can't afford not to think about Managing Differently. Here's why.

First, while an organization's energy for diversity as an initiative may increase or diminish over time, the need to get the best from all employees is a constant. As long as employees are human, they will be diverse. Therefore, whether you recognize it or not, you are faced with the challenges of Managing Differently—so you might as well be as effective at it as you can!

Second, most organizations recognize that the world is changing. It's evident in the marketplace, the customer base, and the pool of potential employees. I think these organizations will increasingly look for managers who demonstrate competence in getting the best from all employees. Whether these organizations call it Managing Differently or something else, the skill of tapping employee talent will be all the more valuable. Are you going to be one of these managers?

Third, although the trend may be to see the psychological contract between employee and employer as exchange-based (i.e., here's what I'll give and here's what I expect, and I'll stay as long as my needs are being met), I know that trust and loyalty are just as important as they have ever been. I also believe that trust and loyalty have a positive impact on bottom-line results because employees who trust their managers are willing to give their best and go the extra mile.

If you make the commitment to be an effective diversity manager, then in the long run, you will be a better manager. You will find greater personal fulfillment as someone who has been able to see the best in people and develop relationships with them. You will also develop a track record as someone who people want to work for and who gets results. So, the choice to be an effective diversity manager is yours. If you choose to pursue this path, then read on. The next section tells you how.

What You Need to Know

1. Your job as a manager is already pretty tough.
2. The need to get the best from all employees is constant.
3. Organizations will increasingly look for managers who demonstrate competence in getting the best from all employees.
4. Employees who trust their managers are willing to give their best and go the extra mile.
5. The choice to be an effective diversity manager is yours.

Reflection

- Do you sometimes feel that your plate is already full, so having to focus on managing your organization's diversity is an additional burden?
- Are you hoping that "all this diversity" will eventually go away?
- Are you interested in becoming a better manager?

PART TWO

Becoming an Effective Diversity Manager

CHAPTER FOUR

The Managing Differently Mind-Set

M anaging Differently is a learned ability. It means being able to identify how each individual works best and adapting your managerial style to that individual. It means increasing your ability to be flexible and your willingness to adapt how you perform certain managerial functions in the interest of increased individual employee and organizational effectiveness.

The basic underlying premise of the Managing Differently model is that for whatever reason, *we tend to find ourselves managing in a fairly narrow range of behaviors.* This range represents our most comfortable way of doing things. We act without thinking. I refer to this as our "natural style." We tend to manage all of our employees as if they were the same, that is, having the same skills and talents, being motivated by the same things, responding to the same incentives, and so on.

In the past, it may have been useful and effective to adopt a single management style and to apply it consistently with all the people you support. In today's workplace, managers must learn to "manage to the individual," which means getting to know

A manager's job is *to get 100 percent from 100 percent of his employees 100 percent of the time.*

people and treating each person the way he or she wants (and needs) to be treated. The challenges that we face require us to try to expand our range, even in situations and organizations where there may not seem to be a lot of latitude.

The desired outcome or objective of Managing Differently is to get results. You should expect to have employees who are confident and competent to perform. Therefore, effective diversity managers help people manage themselves by focusing consistently on performance and results, and by allowing them to think in their own unique way about getting those results.

The message in Managing Differently is that we each have different approaches to work that are most likely to result in optimal levels of performance. These approaches are not good or bad; they are just different. The manager's job is *to get 100 percent from 100 percent of her employees 100 percent of the time* by understanding and adapting to the employees' approaches to work—not the other way around. As a manager, you may have to identify and then be willing to expand your own comfort zones and go beyond your preferences. You must take advantage of the existing set of skills, methods, tools, and philosophies that you have already learned about management and then apply these tools differently for different people in different situations at different times.

Managing Differently is not a set of prescribed behaviors. Instead, it is a mind-set, a commitment to equity (i.e. fairness, impartiality, justice). It calls for you, as a manager, to be conscious, alert, and aware of each interface with each employee that you support. Doing what comes naturally can have unintended consequences. Doing what is equitable requires thought, diligence, and discipline. The Managing Differently model, principles, and tools discussed in this section help you develop that discipline.

The Managing Differently Model

The ultimate goal of Managing Differently is to be able to seamlessly move from your natural style to an adaptive style according to the situation. You need not apply robotic skills. Instead, the model challenges you to think about your role as a manager in your behavior with each employee.

The Managing Differently model illustrates this new challenge. It represents the fact that we all tend to have a natural or preferred management style. That style evolves over time but basically represents how we think we are most effective at managing people. By understanding the components of the model, you will be better prepared to spot a management challenge and respond to it effectively.

Managing Differently Model

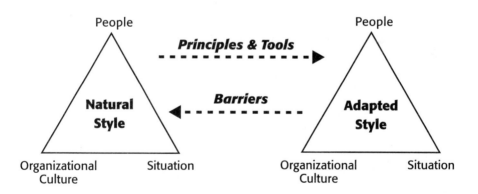

The model illustrates three main factors that influence your behavior as a manager: people, organizational culture, and situation. As a manager, you have a choice to use your natural style of management or an adaptive style of management for any given interaction. The three influencers are referenced as points of the triangle. Keep in mind that there are other influencers such as level of expertise, education, and executive support, but the three I reference have proven to be the most important and sometimes the most challenging when it comes to managerial behavior. Principles and tools help you adapt while barriers keep you from moving seamlessly between the two modes. The influencers (people, organizational culture, and situation) are discussed in the remainder of this chapter. The other factors (barriers, principles, and tools) are discussed in subsequent chapters.

People

The first of these influencers is our perception of people and their perceptions of us. The critical elements include how you view yourself in the role of manager; how you view others, particularly employees; and how they view you. Each one of us is a composite of the diversity dimensions that we represent. These dimensions, individually and collectively, have a great deal to do with how we perceive the world. Oddly enough, the most obvious dimensions of diversity are quite often the least informative. Knowing that someone is white, male, and over fifty may not be as useful in assessing his needs, desires, motivations, talent, and expectations as knowing that he was raised on a Midwestern farm, is a devout follower of an unusual spiritual group, has eight children, and was a military officer.

As managers—and human beings—we develop our perceptions of others very rapidly and usually within a short time of meeting them. Once formed, these perceptions lock us into a way of interacting with others based on our perceptions, and we find it difficult to acknowledge new information about the other person, especially when it challenges our perception. *Managing Differently requires that we suspend our perceptions of others and allow ourselves to seek new information about them—particularly our employees.*

Think about the employees in your work group. If you had to describe each one in five words or less, what would you say?

How different are your descriptions from the impressions that you formed of these employees when you first met them? What do you think about the employees in your work group? Do you see them as tools for your use, or students under your tutelage, or warm bodies, or chess pieces that you move around? Do you see them as fellow workers with a different job assignment than yours? Have you prejudged some of the employees in your group? Do you think of some of them as stars and others as duds?

The challenge in Managing Differently is not one of stopping ourselves from forming perceptions, which would be impossible, given how we as humans process information. However, Managing Differently does require you to be willing to continuously test the accuracy of your perceptions by seeking new information (through interaction and relationship-building) and allowing your perceptions to change.

Organizational Culture

Organizations often have implicit messages on the appropriate ways to do things (unwritten rules of behavior). Although they are unspoken, most people in the organization quickly internalize these rules and recognize the need to comply. The point is that we often do not act in the workplace the same way we would at home or at a baseball game. Now, I know that represents duplicity. I also know that it takes place every day at every organization on the face of the earth. To take it further, what is appropriate and accepted behavior in one organization is not acceptable in another. Think about the difference in dress codes between a Silicon Valley technology company and the U.S. Army.

Organizational culture is a major determinant of managerial behavior. Oftentimes, its influence operates at an unconscious level, so we act in ways consistent with the cultural norms without thinking about it. For example, my associates and I have encountered many organizations with conflict-averse cultures. Unfortunately, over time, this approach has been interpreted as "don't be the bearer of bad news" and "don't rock the boat." Managers in conflict-averse cultures may find it personally and professionally difficult to give (and receive) candid feedback. Managing Differently requires giving employees straightforward feedback, so they either can make adjustments in their performance or help you to see the benefit of their ways.

The challenge for you as a manager is to be aware of the culture of your organization, so you can choose your behaviors appropriately (i.e., adapt). I find that managers who stay grounded in the belief that their primary responsibility is to get 100 percent from their employees find ways to operate within the culture and oftentimes to influence shifts in their organization's culture because of the results they achieve.

Situation

The third influencer in the behavior triangle of the model is situation. This refers to the context in which your particular work group operates. Any number of variables describe the situation. For example, working on an assembly line is very different than working in research and development. Some work situations are crisis-driven, demanding immediate response to anything that occurs. The time horizon is fairly short. Other situations are more long-range in nature. Projects may go on for eons before completion. There may be few fire drills. Some situations involve being isolated, meaning that the work can be completed with very little interaction with others outside of the work group. Other situations are highly interactive. The only way to complete one's work is by gathering, involving, or interacting with a lot of other people.

Many different situations exist within the same organization. On any given day, and sometimes during the same day, you may be faced with a steady-state (routine) work situation, a state of intense activity, or a crisis. Each of these situations influences the range of behaviors in which you will engage. From the Managing Differently perspective, I encourage you to look for opportunities to seek employees' contributions while keeping in mind what is not warranted because of the nature of the operations. For example, a manager in a nuclear power plant may have fewer opportunities for engaging and acknowledging diverse ideas and opinions than a manager of a creative team in an ad agency. (However, keep in mind that Managing Differently opportunities exist in all work environments, including nuclear power plants!)

What You Need to Know

1. You can learn to manage differently.
2. The objective of Managing Differently is to get results.
3. Doing what comes naturally can have unintended consequences.
4. Your management behavior is influenced by your perception of people, your organization's culture, and the situation.

Reflection

- How narrow is your management style?
- Who are your stars? Who are your duds?
- Describe your organization's culture in five words or less. What does it require you to do as a manager? Does it allow you to be effective with all your employees?
- Do you manage the same in all situations?

CHAPTER FIVE

Barriers

S aying we must be adaptive is one thing. Doing it is another. Some barriers you must overcome in order to make adaptiveness a natural part of your behavior are *preferences, comfort, traditions,* and *distractions.*

Preferences

You are a manager, yet you are still human. As a human, you are subject to the same conditioning as all other humans. You have a set of experiences that have shaped who you are and how you view the world. You tend to prefer and appreciate people you know, like, and trust, which is natural. Moreover, you tend to know, like, and trust people who most nearly mirror those attributes that you see in yourself and have come to value. The list of preferences is different for each manager. They may be self-starters (because you are a self-starter), tall and slim (because all of your business heroes are tall and slim), or loquacious (because you come from a family of talkers). Whatever the attribute and whatever the source of the preference, you must acknowledge that you like it when you see it, and you are somewhat put off when you don't. The attribute affects your perception of people. However, your preferences are not requirements.

Comfort

If ever there were a concept that is hard to describe, it is comfort. How do you describe what makes you comfortable? You put words to it, and it seems somehow elitist, exclusionary, and biased. Yet, you know it when you feel it. Comfort is a very personal matter.

For example, when you shop for a new mattress for your bed, inevitably you will sit on the mattress, perhaps lie on it, even bounce on it before making the purchase decision. Why not just base your decision on the specifications, the features and benefits, and the price? Well, I would suggest that you are not really buying a king-sized, triple-coiled, premium-rated mattress with interlacing padding. Instead, you are buying a comfortable way to rest at night, and you know it when you feel it. Furthermore, once you have broken that mattress in and have grown used to how it feels, letting go of that mattress is hard. My wife and I slept on the same mattress for over twenty years. We finally changed, but only after the original mattress collapsed from being used as a trampoline by our grandkids.

As managers, we also become comfortable with routines and styles. We test them out as they are being developed. We observe others, we try our hand at certain techniques, we wait to see the results we get, and then we conclude that what we are doing either works or not. If it works, we have just officially adopted a management style. And like a good mattress, once we grow used to that style, letting go is hard. Usually, we change only if something breaks or there is another compelling reason to change.

> Left to your natural self, you prefer to work with and to have relationships with "your kind of people."

Traditions

A tradition is a long-standing custom or practice that has the effect of an unwritten law. Traditions are powerful in their influence on behavior. Almost unconsciously, managers try to "act like managers." Quite often, acting like a manager means doing what managers have always done. What is interesting is that new managers fall into tradition-bound behavior even when they had openly opposed that behavior in other managers. Here's an example of what I mean by tradition-bound behavior:

> One of our client organizations has a tradition that allocates space based on level. First-line supervisors are given cubicles of a certain size and a chair with arms. Managers are given an office with a door. As such, managers are expected to "hold court" in their office.
>
> In our work with this organization we noticed one of the supervisors who was known for walking around and interacting informally with the members of his team. This behavior made him very popular and very effective with his employees. However, once he was promoted to the next level, he received an office. This same supervisor who had been known for walking around stopped doing it. He had begun to honor the tradition of managers at his company, which said, "As a manager, people are supposed to come see you, not the other way around."

Distractions

The final thing that keeps us from moving gracefully and effortlessly from our natural style to an adaptive style is distractions. Each day, there are at least a hundred things to distract our thoughts and consume our attention. Sometimes it feels like a million! As you are attempting to learn and practice new behaviors for managing people, you must contend with all these distractions. When you are distracted, of course, you naturally lapse back into your uncon-scious, natural (preferred) way of doing things.

One of the biggest distractions managers face is the endless list of busy work they are required to perform: going to meet-ings, writing reports, appeasing their managers, and the paper-work—oh, the paperwork. All these activities distract managers from their core job: to encourage, develop, and support people.

• • • •

These barriers are not insurmountable. What is required is a clear commitment to the 100 percent imperative.

What You Need to Know

1. Preferring and appreciating people like yourself is natural.
2. Your preferences do not constitute requirements.
3. Your comfort is a very personal thing and may not be a good measure of performance.
4. Indulging your preferences, avoiding discomfort, adhering to tradition, or giving in to distractions can all cause you to lapse back to your natural way of doing things and to focus away from getting the best from each of your people.

Reflection

- What attributes do you like in people? Do you use them to judge performance?
- What would cause you to change your style?
- Do you try to act like a manager? What does that mean to you?

CHAPTER SIX

Managing Differently Principles

As I stated earlier, the primary goal of Managing Differently is to get *100 percent from 100 percent of your employees 100 percent of the time.* Yet many managers are content with finding their "best" employees and riding them to victory while pulling the stragglers along for the ride—or hoping that they will go elsewhere. The best employees are often described as "self-starters," "results-oriented," "achievers," "stars," and "high potentials." In reality, they tend to be those people who the manager *knows, likes, and trusts.* Anyone who is too "different" will have a hard time making the cut in this environment.

Effective diversity managers strive to get the best from all employees. No stragglers allowed. Everyone is a star. Sound impossible? When I was working with Total Quality Management (TQM) and suggested 100 percent targets for quality or customer satisfaction, most of my clients were in total disbelief. They said, "No can do! It's crazy to try. You must not understand how things are done around here. At best we can hope to get 80 percent from 20 percent of our employees and to drag whatever we can from the rest."

Yet, with the unreasonable goal of 100 percent quality came unexpected gains in productivity, breakthrough thinking about process improvement, and record business achievements. Has anyone achieved 100 percent quality? Only occasionally. The value is in the *striving.*

Accomplishing the 100 percent imperative requires you to engage in *principle-driven behavior.* Giving you prescriptions for responding to every situation that you will encounter with your employees is impossible. What I can share with you is a set of principles to guide you as you learn about their differences and develop relationships with each of them. I have worded them as "I" statements to help you internalize them.

Principle 1   **I believe every employee can give 100 percent. My responsibility is to help them do it.**

Principle 2   **As a manager, I bear a greater responsibility for developing relationships with my employees.**

Principle 3   **I am responsible for understanding and managing my own dimensions of diversity and my reactions to differences.**

Principle 4   **I must adapt my style and behavior to get the best from each employee.**

Principle 5   **I have the power and ability to provide what my employees need from me.**

Accomplishing the 100 percent imperative requires you to engage in principle-driven behavior.

Principle 6   **Each employee knows how he/she wants to be treated. If I want to know, I have to ask.**

Principle 7   **Treating people equally and fairly does not mean treating them the same.**

Each principle is discussed in detail.

Principle 1   **I believe every employee can give 100 percent. My responsibility is to help them do it.**

Psychologists have demonstrated time and time again that our thoughts can become self-fulfilling prophecies. What we think about other people influences our behavior towards them, which in turn elicits a reaction or response from them that often confirms our original belief. This process happens unconsciously, and we often don't recognize that we started the process by our thoughts and beliefs. This process often elicits negative behavior, but it can also be used for the opposite effect. If we believe that people are capable of giving their best, we will treat them as if they can—and that's what we are likely to get. Remember the words of Peter Drucker: "the role of an effective manager is to make each employee's strengths effective and her weaknesses irrelevant."[9]

Every employee has strengths and weaknesses. Surely, if you think hard enough, you can name some weaknesses of your best employee and some strengths of your worst employee. Based on experience, you will, of course, make assignments based on abilities and proven success. I'm simply saying that you should also be aware of the labels you unfairly place on your employees. Perhaps you've simply never seen a black woman excel in this particular role, or perhaps you've yet to see a clerk transition successfully into the role of lead accountant. That doesn't mean it can't happen.

Principle 2	**As a manager, I bear a greater responsibility for developing relationships with my employees.**

Managers have tremendous impact on the quality and productivity of an employee's work life. Managers must come to understand that their major reason for being (their personal mission) is to support the people whom they are assigned to manage. Such responsibility means making sure that each person has everything he/she needs to be effective, including: equipment, supplies, skills, knowledge, training, developmental assignments, encouragement, empowerment, recognition, and motivation. This requires you to develop a relationship with each employee. The challenge is that this may be more difficult with employees who are not like you because you don't share a common ground from which to start. For example, you may not come from the same part of the country, you may not have the same educational experiences, you may have come from different parts of the company, you may not share the same racial or ethnic background, or you may be of different genders.

Taking the initiative in forming this relationship is your responsibility. You don't have to like each employee, and they don't have to like you. Your job is to get the best from each employee by having a relationship based on respect and appreciation. If you fail to develop a supportive working relationship, misperceiving each other can interfere with your effectiveness and theirs.

Principle 3 **I am responsible for understanding and managing my own dimensions of diversity and reactions to differences.**

In the process of being sensitive to and responding to the unique needs of your diverse employees, remember that you, too, are a human being. You are also driven and influenced by the things that make you unique. Therefore, you must learn to manage your own "stuff" if you are ever to be able to manage each employee in a unique way. Your perceptions and assumptions are influenced by your dimensions of diversity and will certainly affect the way you respond to others. A great philosopher once said, *"We see things not as they are but as we are."*

Remember all of the different diversity dimensions that we each bring to the work place. These dimensions—combined with our perceptions of ourselves, others, the organization, and the situation—influence our management behaviors. You can easily mistake your perceptions for absolute facts. Remember that your perceptions are simply that: perceptions—a result of your upbringing, experiences, and the messages you've internalized. Learning to observe objectively can lead you closer to the actual facts.

I have observed how some managers respond when they encounter someone who they perceive to be different. Almost by impulse, they place the onus on the other person to make them comfortable. They expect that person to learn to assimilate and be more like everyone else. As an effective diversity manager, you need to take responsibility for your own perceptions and reactions and to constantly challenge yourself to test their accuracy.

Principle 4 **I must adapt my style and behavior to get the best from each employee.**

We are all more creative and productive when we are allowed to just be ourselves. Working with others requires some adjustment and accommodation from everyone. The more adjustments that take place, the more productivity we lose. Therefore, it only makes sense that if one person, the manager, adjusts more and allows the others to adjust less, we will have better outcomes.

As I stated earlier, we tend to manage in a fairly narrow range of behaviors. We tend to manage all of our employees as if they were the same—had the same skills and talents, were motivated by the same things, responded to the same incentives, and so on. The management style you adopt is no accident. It is the sum total of your temperament, education, experience, and preferences. Much of your style is learned from people that you admire, like company leaders or former managers. It stands to reason that you really believe that your adopted style is the right way to manage people. After all, it worked on you.

In order to get full contribution from every employee and allow every employee to reach his maximum potential, you as the manager have to develop a more adaptive style that takes into account the changing environment you work in and the diversity of the people you support.

A great example of adaptation occurs in the movie *A League of Their Own* about a World War II–era women's major league baseball team. Tom Hanks plays the team manager, Jimmy Dugan. He had been the home run champ for two years in the major leagues. He had been raised playing baseball and he had played at every level. He had coached, and now he was a manager. Jimmy Dugan knew baseball and baseball culture. One of the things he knew was how to respond when a player made a fundamental error on the field. He knew that it was his job as manager to yell and harangue the player mercilessly until they realized their mistake and committed to get it right.

Jimmy became the coach and manager for a women's baseball team. In one scene, Jimmy is caught doing his duty by screaming at the centerfielder, who had just made the mistake of missing the cutoff man during a routine base hit. As a result of her error, a run had scored. But something unusual happens that gets Jimmy's attention. While he is chastising the centerfielder with every expletive he could muster up, she responds by bursting into tears and losing her confidence. This behavior causes him to respond with the classic line, "There's no crying in baseball!" Needless to say, Jimmy did not get the result he was looking for.

In a later scene, Jimmy is faced with the same situation with the same player. This time, however, instead of using his natural style, he uses a calm and reasoned approach with the centerfielder. He explains the impact of the error. He discusses his expectations for future performance, and he does so without raising his voice. As a result the centerfielder acknowledged the coaching, committed to improving her performance, and even thanked Jimmy for the intervention. Watching the video makes it clear how hard it was for Jimmy to manage differently. You can see the pain on his face as he adapts his style; it was killing him. But the final outcome was the result he wanted. Similar to this scenario, your responsibility is to adapt your style and find the ways that get each of your employees to respond with better results.

Principle 5   I have the power and ability to provide what my employees need from me.

If you are truly open to encouraging, supporting, and developing all the people to whom you are assigned, you may be concerned about your ability to meet all their needs. Budgets are tight. Raises are small. Promotions are few. Company policies are being enforced closely. How can you hope to provide what employees need from you when they ask? I recommend that you remember that your employees also know the facts of the business. They are not likely to request something of you that cannot be accomplished by someone in your position. If they do, treat them like adults. Review the facts and ask them to help you figure out how to do what they are asking, given the facts.

On some level, I think many managers feel powerless because they are caught between higher-ups and employees. The reality is that you have all the power you need to develop supportive relationships with your employees. You don't need permission to sit down and talk to them.

Principle 6	**Each employee knows how he/she wants to be treated. If I want to know, I have to ask.**

People are usually willing and able to solve their own problems and provide input for their own needs. You have to be willing to let them. One of the great freedoms that comes with Managing Differently is to release yourself from the obligation to always have the answer. Instead, your role is to help employees find the answer by careful questioning, probing, and coaching.

Principle 7	**Treating people equally and fairly does not mean treating them the same.**

Contrary to popular belief, preferential treatment is a desirable behavior for managers as long as everyone on the team receives it. Letting everyone know that you are attempting to respond to their needs based on what you know about them, not by following the book, is absolutely necessary. When you attempt to create the perception of fairness by treating everyone the same, you inevitably create a perception of unfairness.

Translating Principles into Behavior

While simply giving you a list of things to do to become an effective diversity manager would be an easy approach, I resist the temptation. To be effective, you do not need to learn to do things in a prescribed manner. More important is that you understand what you are trying to achieve with your behaviors. How will you know what to do if you only have a principle? Let's look at an example.

Suppose you were having one of those days where everything is going wrong. To add to the problem, you just had a disturbing call from home that made you distracted and angry. One of your employees is young, playful, brash, and haughty, and looks a little like that disrespectful, unkempt guy who tried to date your daughter two years ago. If that employee pops into your office and asks to leave work early for some unspecified reason, how will you respond? Let's assume also that you had just let another employee, Mary, leave early the day before, and everyone saw it. I can almost guess how you would like to respond.

However, you remember that your very purpose as a manager is to get 100 percent performance from all of your employees (Principle 1). Principle 7 reminds you that treating everyone equally does not mean treating them the same. Just remembering those principles may cause you to spare the young man's life and really listen to his request in an attempt to understand his need and to give a fair and equitable response. By the way, that response may not be to let him leave as you had let Mary leave. In Managing Differently, we advocate giving employees preferential treatment, as long as *all employees* receive the preferential treatment. Your response to this employee should be based on your understanding of his unique situation and needs, and not by the precedent set with another employee. You should also be able to explain your decision in a way that helps everyone feel okay about it.

In this example, principles influence behavior. As you can imagine, doing it well may require some behavioral skills that may not currently be a part of your toolkit. You perhaps should begin learning new ways to say and do things so that the people you support will appreciate your attempts to manage more equitably.

You Will Make Mistakes

In learning to manage differently, challenges can creep into your work life when you least expect it. Even the most experienced and talented manager can expect to make mistakes now and then. Guess what? You're human. You have blind spots like everyone else. Start now to include a lot of diverse allies around you and to recognize that it's okay to say, "I blew it. Thank you for the feedback. I'm going to do better."

What You Need to Know

1. Getting 100 percent from 100 percent of your people 100 percent of the time involves grounding your behavior in the principles of Managing Differently.

2. The Managing Differently Principles are:

Principle 1   I believe every employee can give 100 percent. My responsibility is to help them do it.

Principle 2   As a manager, I bear a greater responsibility for developing relationships with my employees.

Principle 3   I am responsible for understanding and managing my own dimensions of diversity and my reactions to differences.

Principle 4   I must adapt my style and behavior to get the best from each employee.

Principle 5   I have the power and ability to provide what my employees need from me.

Principle 6   Each employee knows how he/she wants to be treated. If I want to know, I have to ask.

Principle 7   Treating people equally and fairly does not mean treating them the same.

3. You will make mistakes as you internalize the principles. Congratulations! That means you're human!

Reflection

- Think of examples where you have demonstrated the principles.
- Think of an opportunity that you missed by not practicing the principles.

CHAPTER SEVEN

Managing Differently Tools

Principles are necessary to guide your behavior as a diversity manager. But you also need to have tools at your disposal. In this section, I discuss three simple tools that I know to be useful:

1. The Managing Differently *Dialogue.*
2. The Belief System.
3. The three-second pause.

The Managing Differently Dialogue

Your effectiveness at managing diversity is highly dependent on one key factor: how well you know your employees. The Managing Differently *Dialogue* is a tool to help you accomplish this. Mastering Managing Differently is virtually impossible if you are not willing to treat each person as a valuable human being worthy of your time and your support. Each person is different. Each

> Your effectiveness at managing diversity is highly dependent on one key factor: how well you know your employees.

person has a unique set of talents and a unique pattern of behaviors, passions, and yearnings. Each person has a unique contribution to make. As the manager, you have to make it a priority to discover and understand each person's uniqueness.

Some of you will protest, "How can I possibly keep track of each employee's unique needs?" Who can blame you? It's hard to treat each employee differently, particularly given that outward appearance offers few clues to an individual's particular needs. It's a little like being told to play chess without knowing how all the pieces move. But the best managers have the solution: Ask.

Ask your employee about her goals:

- What are you shooting for in your current role?
- Where do you see your career heading?
- What personal goals would you feel comfortable sharing with me?
- How often do you want to meet to talk about your progress?

Ask how she would like to receive feedback. Does she seem to like public recognition or private? Written or verbal? Who is her best audience? It can be very effective to ask her to tell you about the most meaningful recognition she has ever received. Find out what made it so memorable. Also, ask her about her relationship with you. Can she tell you how she learns? You might inquire whether she has ever had any mentors or partners who have helped her, and if so, how they helped.

Without knowledge of your employees you are functionally blind, flailing around with stereotypes, generalizations, and misguided notions that "fairness" means "sameness." But armed with knowledge, you are focused. You can focus on each person's strengths and turn talents into performance.

The Managing Differently Dialogue, which is the first step in managing your diverse workforce more effectively, is designed as a formal way to perform an informal task. Ideally, a manager should maintain constant awareness of each employee's needs, but you still have to start somewhere. With this tool, you will understand more about what makes the individuals on your team tick. The dialogue provides a structured and proven way to get the information you need. Of course, the climate, timing, and level of trust are important to the process.

Now, for all of you who are getting butterflies in your stomach thinking, "I can't do this!" let me assure you that I provide advice and tools so you can feel comfortable sitting down with your employees and discussing these questions. I am also providing you with some skills that you can use in doing the interview.

When something is hard, focusing on the expected outcomes or objectives can help. The *objectives* for the dialogue are

- To understand what motivates each individual in the group
- To uncover how each person likes to receive feedback
- To encourage two-way communication
- To begin to create an environment where discussing issues of diversity is okay
- To *improve your effectiveness as a manager* by getting feedback on your strengths and weaknesses

Again, *this conversation is designed for your benefit, to help you improve. The dialogue is not the time for you to counsel employees on how they should behave.*

When seeking information from your employees about the conditions that will help them reach peak performance, remember, *preparation is everything.* Plan the timing and climate for the employee discussion and let your direct reports know in advance about the conversation and its purpose. In addition, attend to the following details to make the conversation successful:

- Set up times to meet with each individual. Block about ninety minutes for the first meeting with each person.
- Assure the individual that your conversation is private and will not be shared with others.

- Let the individual know that you may jot down some notes because you hope this session will help you become a more effective manager.
- Try to make the person feel comfortable and understand that whatever he says will not be held against him in any way. A little self-disclosure may also help.
- Be prepared to listen and observe. This is not the time for you to defend the company or your position. It is a time to gather information that will help you manage your diverse group more effectively.
- Listen for clues that the employee has beliefs that are limiting his motivation to perform.

Below are some sample questions to give you an idea of the types of things a manager should know about her employees. Experiment with these questions and the responses they generate until you get the answers you need to help you support each employee you manage. Practice until this process becomes natural and spontaneous.

At the beginning of each year, or a week or two after someone has been hired, spend the time with him saying, "You know, John, I'm your manager. I want to be the best possible manager for you. So, I need your help." To borrow a phrase from the movie *Jerry Maguire*, "Help me help you." Then, ask the following questions:

1. "Tell me a little about your work experience so far at the company." (Use this to open up the discussion. The employee can tell you as much or as little as he would like about his experience at your company.)

2. "What do you like most about your current position?"

3. "What do you like the least about your current position?"

4. "Are there any policies/practices at the company that concern you? What are they?"

5. "Are there talents or skills that you have that could be better utilized here?"

6. "If you could change one thing about your current working environment, what would it be?"

7. "What is it that you want but are not getting enough of at work?" (Examples: praise, respect, feedback, recognition, clarity, prestige, authority, balance, affiliation, time off, caring boss, pride in team's work, etc.)

8. "When you think about all of the work you have done or projects you have been a part of in and outside of work, what have you enjoyed most? What have you enjoyed least?"

9. "In what ways do you feel different at our company?"

10. "What things do I now say or do that have a positive impact on your motivation and performance?"

11. "What things do I say or do that have caused you to hold back your motivation and performance?"

12. "What are some things that I could start doing right away that could improve your motivation and performance?"

13. "What are the things you most want me to know and understand about you? What things are you most reluctant to discuss?"

14. "Nobody does everything well. We are all uncomfortable with some parts of our job. What are the things that are most difficult for you to do?"

15. "How could I be a better, more supportive manager for you?"

16. "Is there anything else you would like to discuss?"

These questions are intended to illustrate the types of things that you should know about each of your employees in order to have a better understanding of her needs and how to be most effective in your role as manager. Practice these questions until they becomes natural, until they seem spontaneous and seamless. *However, remember that the responses are more important than the questions.* Use them to *establish a dialogue.* As managers become more effective at this questioning, they learn that they can often get all of the information they need with just a few of the questions. Listening and facilitation skills become very important here. An "oh?" "tell me more about that," "what would you like to see happen differently?" or "what did you like/not like about that?" will lead an employee to reveal much more about herself and, of course, how she wants to be managed.

The Managing Differently Dialogue gives you more clues about how you can better support your employees. The intent is to help you as a manager adapt to each employee instead of making each employee adapt to you.

Now, many of you will be concerned about having a conversation like this with each employee. Own up to those concerns and mentally dispel them one-by-one. Some of the most common concerns are:

1. If I ask, the person may not answer honestly. What can I do to promote honest dialogue?

   Answer: To start an open dialogue, you must first be open. People are less likely to be self-revealing if you approach them coldly and without feeling. Make it clear that these inquiries are intended to help you be a more effective manager for them.

2. If I ask, the person may tell me honestly and it may be uncomfortable to hear. How can I prepare so that I can manage my own feelings?

   Answer: Suck it up. If you know you have been less than effective in the past, be prepared to hear it from your employees. Some people soften the blow with polite words, while others delight in letting you have it between the eyes. Remember your goal to get information that will help you improve. He who has a "why" can endure almost any "what" or "how."

3. If I ask, the person may request something I can't deliver. How will I respond?

> Answer: Relax. The people you are talking to are mature, responsible adults. They are not likely to ask for something beyond your scope of authority. They will, however, help remind you that you can do a lot more than you are accustomed to doing to support your team.

4. If I ask, I may appear vulnerable and not in control. Is that okay?

> Answer: Being vulnerable is a fundamental principle of leadership. People help you when you make it clear that you need help. If you come across as having it all together, they figure you don't need their input and they withhold their support. Remember, *no one cares how much you know until they know how much you care.*

The Managing Differently Dialogue is not a one-time conversation. While you may have regularly scheduled opportunities to talk (e.g., annually), you should have informal dialogue taking place on an ongoing basis.

The Three Beliefs

Performance can only be managed if you, the manager, understand the factors that cause performance to soar or lapse. It is clear from extensive research that performance is driven by the motivation to perform. Furthermore, the motivation to perform is controlled by beliefs—believe it or not! That's right, it matters little what YOU are doing or not doing to promote high performance. It only matters what your people believe. So, if you can find a way to determine what people believe and if you can help manage those beliefs, you are in a better position to manage performance.

According to Dr. Thad Green of The Belief System Institute,[10] there are three essential belief areas that relate to job performance. In order to deliver quality performance, each person must have positive beliefs in each of these areas. The first belief (B-1) is about confidence: the person has to believe she is capable of performing the task. For example, if I asked my son, a psychology major, to work real hard to get an A in a thermonuclear physics class I happened to enroll him in, I doubt that he would achieve the goal or put in much effort toward the goal. He has no reason to believe that his effort would produce the desired outcome. He would have a legitimate (B-1) problem of low confidence.

The second essential belief (B-2) has to do with trust. People must believe that performance matters. This means that they must believe that performance and only performance will be the basis for rewards or punishment. Are your employees given outcomes (praise, reprimand, bonuses, pay cuts, extra work, time off) based solely on performance? If not, why should they believe that performance matters? For example, many people of color and women believe their progress and quality relationships are affected not by performance, but by cronyism, good ol' boys, or unwritten rules of acceptability. At the same time, many white men believe that their progress and quality relationships are affected by diversity programs, quotas, Affirmative Action targets, and reverse discrimination. With these beliefs in mind, employees are less likely to commit themselves to high levels of performance because they believe there is no reward. Where did these employees get these ideas? Quite simply, they learned by watching manager behavior.

The third essential belief (B-3) has to do with employees' satisfaction with performance incentives. People have to believe that the rewards or punishment you give for performance matter to them. Does your company have a standard set of incentives for performance (spot bonuses, all-expense-paid trip to Cleveland, etc.)? What about your personal recognition scheme? Is it limited to congratulations, lunch with the boss, or more work? Remember, it doesn't matter if you have the most sophisticated incentive plan ever devised if none of the rewards are of interest to your employee. People are not likely to work hard for something they don't want.

The three beliefs outlined above are all part of a process called *The Belief System of Motivation and Performance*™:

Three Conditions for Motivation and Performance

B-1	Confidence	"I can do it."
B-2	Trust	"I believe I will be rewarded for my performance."
B-3	Satisfaction	"I believe I will like what I get."

Remember that all three beliefs must be positive to achieve high levels of performance.

I believe that if you can understand and master the concepts in this system, you will become a more effective diversity manager. You will be able to manage performance rather than just monitor it. Using the three beliefs allows you to quickly identify a performance problem, to determine the cause of the problem, and to execute a solution. That's performance management. Try this. If you have an employee who is not performing to expectation, have a brief discussion with them using the Belief System concepts. I like to start with B-3 and move up to B-1 because it is easier for people to confirm B-3 and B-2 problems than to admit B-1 problems. Ask:

- Am I giving you things (praise, freebies, etc.) that you want? (B-3)
- Are there things that you want but are not getting? (B-3)
- Have I been consistent in rewarding performance in our work group or do you see other things affecting rewards? Does this matter to you? (B-2)

If these questions don't help you address the issue, then ask:

- Are you confident you know how to complete this assignment? If not, what are you missing? How can I help? (B-1)

Of course, you can only pull this off if you are able to ask your employees for honest information about their performance and get a complete answer. That is why the Managing Differently Dialogue is so important. It gives you a tool to develop a relationship and then, when necessary, investigate each employee's Belief System with the understanding that it will be different for each one.

The Three-Second Pause

Managing Differently Principle 3 says that you are responsible for managing your own perceptions and reactions to differences because they influence your behavior. Whenever you encounter a new person or a new situation, you can be sure that your *little voice* will have something to say. The little voice is inside your head and is quick to offer opinions. This "background conversation" may be going on even as you are saying the opposite to this new person.

The little voice is judgmental, opinionated, irrational, illogical, and does not care if it tells you the truth. The little voice thinks it knows everything about everything and everybody. You have to realize when this little voice is going on in your head and how it may affect your interactions with others.

The messages from your little voice are informed and influenced by your background and how you were "socially programmed" in the past. The way you use this information determines how you react to people. How do you think "social programming" influences your decisions about others in your work group?

> Whenever you encounter a new person or a new situation, you can be sure that your *little voice* will have something to say.

The problem is that you process this information quickly and unconsciously. The result is that you can go from thought to behavior so fast that you often don't realize how or why you reacted the way you did. You are just acting naturally. As I said earlier, acting naturally can have unintended consequences. You may say or do something that is inappropriate or offensive and that damages your relationship with an employee. Or, you may be saying the right thing but your little voice may communicate your true feelings nonverbally. Notice that you have no conscious, malicious intent.

To guard against slipping too hard or too often, I recommend a tool called the *Three-Second Pause*. Surprisingly, in as little as three seconds, you have time to examine your assumptions and modify your reactions so that you can avoid an unnecessary faux pas. During the Three-Second Pause, you should be thinking:

- What am I assuming?
- Why am I assuming that?
- Is it based on old, unexamined perceptions, or is it fresh, real, and validated?
- How am I about to behave? Is that the right thing to do?
- What is the best way to respond to ensure that I am creating a basis for genuine relationship with this person?

The gap between your perception and the current reality indicates the need to examine your assumptions and seek additional information before drawing a conclusion. Your influence on your employees is strong and important. Isn't it worth a few extra seconds to make sure that your influence is positive and respectful? Develop the habit of pausing before you act. Use the Three-Second Pause.

• • • •

These tools (the Managing Differently Dialogue, the Three-Second Pause, and The Belief System) are simple but powerful.

In discussions with managers who have made big "mistakes" with employees and with senior executives, most of them comment that just knowing the person a little better or having the discipline to think about the consequences of their action beforehand could have saved them and their company huge distress and discomfort.

What You Need to Know

1. The better you know each employee, the more effective you'll be at helping each employee achieve her best.
2. The best way to know how to support each employee is to ask each one what works best.
3. The Managing Differently Dialogue is a tool for developing your relationship with each employee while learning what works best for each one.
4. Each time we meet someone or encounter a new situation, our little voice has something to say—and it's usually judgmental or critical.
5. The best way to counteract the little voice is to practice the Three-Second Pause. Take a moment to examine your own assumptions.

Reflection

- What do you do currently to get to know your employees?
- How often has an employee said to you, "I don't think I know how to do that (assignment)?" Is it possible they may be feeling this way but not telling you?
- How would you feel if you discovered that your employees had little trust that their efforts would be rewarded? How would you find out?
- Are you sure you are providing satisfactory incentives for outstanding performance? Who decided what those incentives would be, anyway?
- Have you ever reacted too quickly and regretted what you said?

PART THREE

The Four Phases

The Cycles of Management

Managing Differently suggests that the relationship between an individual employee and her manager is the most important and influential relationship at work. The quality of that relationship can affect the satisfaction, attitude, motivation, creativity, innovation, and productivity of the employee. As you work toward getting the best from each of your employees, you go through a predictable pattern to the cycle of involvement. In each of these phases, you have an opportunity to positively (or negatively) influence the quality of your employees' work life.

The diagram below illustrates the four phases of management that you experience with each employee.

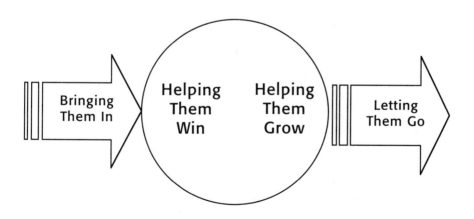

The cycle begins with *Bringing Them In*, when you identify, select, hire, orient, and assign a new employee. The working partnership between you and your employee begins here.

Next, you help your employee perform at peak levels and experience success in her work. This phase, *Helping Them Win*, involves all of the activities that help employees produce outstanding performance results.

Concurrently, you must attend to expanding the skills and abilities, knowledge, and emotional intelligence of each employee. *Helping Them Grow* involves those activities that contribute to the employees' increased potential—that is, the ability to take on greater responsibility and to add even more value to the organization. In this phase, you help the employee prepare for assignments beyond the present one.

Finally, you must prepare and be prepared for the time when the employee moves on to other work. *Letting Them Go* involves those activities that prepare both the employee and the work group for the inevitable parting of the ways.

In each of these phases, the effective diversity manager has primary responsibility for supporting the employees and making sure they have what they individually need to be successful. Each of the phases is discussed in the following chapters.

What You Need to Know

1. The four phases of employee-manager relationships are:
   Bringing Them In,
   Helping Them Win,
   Helping Them Grow, and
   Letting Them Go.

Reflection

• Are you equally effective in all phases, or stronger in some?

CHAPTER NINE

Bringing Them In

The first and, arguably, the most important interaction a manager has with an employee is the selection and hiring process. Selection is not limited to hiring new people into the company. It also includes choosing between internal and external candidates for an open position; selecting a group of people for a special assignment, task force, or committee; or recommending one of your current staff for special development programs.

If you are like other executives and managers, you spend much of your time on managing people and making people decisions. No other decisions are as long-lasting in their consequences or so difficult to unmake, and yet, managers make poor selection, hiring, promotion, and staffing decisions more often than they would like to admit. In fact, by all accounts, managers are successful only one-third of the time in selecting the right people for key jobs. Another third are adequate at best, and the last third are outright failures.

> The most important interaction a manager has with an employee is the selection and hiring process.

The Safe Choice

IBM takes pride in saying that "No one ever got fired for picking IBM as his information technology provider." This statement illustrates one of the barriers you may have in making good selections. You may be inclined to select people who are safe: the known quantity, the one who will not raise questions, the one most like the last incumbent, the one most like you, the one recommended by your boss, and so on. Understanding Principle 3 (managing your own diversity and responses to others' differences) and the barriers are so important in this situation. The problem is that safe selection is not always the best selection. Many people of color and women in organizations complain that they are overlooked for key assignments for this reason.

I overheard a senior executive talking to his peers during an executive training session. He was discussing a recent appointment he made to a field operations job as part of the company's leadership development process. He said, "I had two great candidates, one white and one black. I decided to wait on another opportunity for the black person because this job is in a rural small-town area. And, if I were a black person, I wouldn't want to move out there and take my family away from the city, even for a short stay."

He made what seemed the safe (and compassionate) decision but not necessarily the best decision. In fact, he was not black and should not assume he knew how a black person (or any person) would respond to the offer. Even more important, he should have already known both individuals well enough to understand what their expectations, needs, and career plans required. Unfortunately, decisions like this are made every day without ever bothering to ask the candidates. In this case, by the way, the black candidate was young, brash, ambitious, a strong leader, and a good fit for the company's culture. When asked about the position he had just been passed over for, he responded, "I would love to have been selected. That's just the kind of assignment I need to get a broader view of the company's operations. And since that team has never had a leader who looks like me, it certainly would have broadened their perspective also." That manager left the company six months later. Safe is seldom best.

New Criteria

Okay, time for a little honesty. When a company adopts a diversity strategy, the expectation is usually that more "nontraditional" people will be considered over traditional employees for positions. If the leaders have not been explicit about what that means, middle managers have a lot of room to make bad assumptions and sometimes bad decisions. Even when they have selected the right person for the right reasons, managers often give wrong explanations to the people who were not selected. That creates a negative folklore about the real intent of a Managing Differently strategy.

For example, if you recently selected a female for a key position in your work group—a work group that was until now all-male—you should expect some backlash from males who thought they should have been selected. Think of the principles and then decide how you would explain your choice.

The explanation of your selection on the back end is easier if you are thoughtful, genuine, and honest about your criteria for selection up front. If your intent is to make the best choice (not the safe choice or the "most qualified"), you have to define what "best choice" means. *In today's environment, the best choice should be the person who brings the most added-value to the team, the region, and the company.* Added value may involve more than job skills.

A fiftyish, white male had been invited to interview for five different jobs recently and had not been selected for any of them. He was asked how he felt about the outcomes. He replied, "In all honesty, a part of me is very disappointed because I know I could have been good in those positions. And I thought about the fact that the successful candidates were a younger white male, two white women, a black man, and a Latina woman. Then I began to consider my own values and principles. I have to admit that all of the other candidates were also qualified for those jobs, and the ones who were selected are doing a good job. It just reminds me that there is more competition now. I will have to work harder on getting better. And, I know, my time will come.

This man also admitted that one of the hiring managers had blamed his selection of a woman on the fact we are "doing this diversity stuff, so my hands are tied." Another manager, however, had been very honest and straightforward in saying that "any of the last five candidates would have been a good choice, and diversity was certainly part of the criteria I used to make the final selection." He went on to explain that because of the section of town where they work, the selection of a Latina woman was a strategic decision.

An effective diversity manager will learn to use relevant criteria for selection decisions. *Deliberate diversity of thought, skills, looks, personality, work history, and so on is certainly relevant in today's global workplace.*

Developing Requirements

Relevant criteria begins with clarity on the assignment. Based on the circumstances, a given job description may call for very different assignments. Do not allow yourself to use the same old job posting description. Think about each open position as if it were brand-new to the organization. This position has the potential to make your team stronger or weaker based on your decision. Spend the time where it counts to flush out the right requirements.

You have the right as a manager to demand that the true requirements of the job be met. However, you must also carefully examine your requirements to determine whether they are real requirements or your preferences. Challenge yourself and

the way things are always done. Take a fresh look at your requirements each time you post a job. Is getting to work by 7:00
A.M. really a requirement of the job, or could it be performed
just as well if the candidate arrived by 9:00 A.M.? Is a master's
degree in engineering really necessary, or is that just what the
former employee had?

Determining Fit

A common problem managers incur when faced with the
task of hiring new employees is the issue of "fit." When asked
what they look for in people to play key roles in their organization, nearly all the executives I have queried give a list like this:
team player, takes initiative, honest, trustworthy, loyal, socially
adept, courteous, kind, respectful, etc. The list sounds good to
me. However, underneath these labels, of course, is a gut feel for
"Is this person one of our kind of people?"

You have to acknowledge that many of your criteria for selection are subjective, so you have to be on guard not to let your
blind spots prevent you from seeing what you are looking for in
the candidates (Principle 3).

Unfamiliar Packaging

Based on who you are and how you were raised, you develop
a set of expectations and criteria for acceptance. These are your
preferences. The qualities, traits, and characteristics you prefer
in others are a way of determining how comfortable you are
with them. These traits are very subjective, hard to measure, and
hard to define, yet they are the primary basis for the decisions
you make about other people. A key concept of Managing Differently requires that you learn to recognize the "right stuff"
when it comes in "unfamiliar packaging."

The idea of *unfamiliar packaging* is simply this: You most
easily identify and recognize positive, desirable traits in people

who are most like you. When they come packaged differently, seeing them is more difficult. In order to be effective in making a decision in favor of a person, you must both know what you are looking for and then recognize it when you see it.

The problem, of course, is spotting these characteristics when you see them. Does an honest person only look one way? Do we all demonstrate respect in the same way? These traits are the right stuff, but they are so subjective that we can often miss them when they exist, and we can assume they exist, when they are absent. By definition, diversity is a barrier to this process. Remember, diversity involves both differences and similarities. However, you often have to get over the barrier of differences in order to recognize similarities.

If you catch yourself selecting the same kind of preferred candidate for each position you have available, you should be asking yourself:

Why am I getting the same results?
Have I made the best decision?
What am I overlooking?

Then, if you're bold, ask someone else for their insights on your hiring patterns.

Making the Decision

You can increase your chances of making a good selection. Begin by looking at a number of candidates. Focus on the fit between the person and the assignment. Formal qualifications should be seen only as the ticket to consideration, not the criteria for selection. Think about the match. The central question is, "Are the strengths of this candidate right for this assignment?" Avoid starting your selection process by looking at weaknesses. You cannot build performance on weaknesses.

Recognize that your filters are going to allow you to recognize the required traits in some potential employees and prevent you from seeing them in others. Be deliberate and disciplined about determining who meets those requirements. Be disciplined in the questions that you ask, check your filters, monitor your reactions to candidates, and finally, seek other opinions.

Do your homework. Ask around. One person's sole judgment of another person is of limited value. Everyone has first impressions, prejudices, likes, and dislikes. You need to listen to what other people think. Those who don't share your paradigm of the world can offer the best insight to a candidate's likelihood of success.

Promote Success

Bringing Them In does not end simply with filling an empty position. It is a manager's responsibility to make the new employee successful not only in the first few days and weeks of the job but throughout the manager-employee relationship. This success requires open communication both with the new hire and the existing team.

What You Need to Know

1. *Bringing Them In* includes hiring and promotion as well as selecting people for special projects and assignments.
2. Each job has stated and unstated requirements. You must examine your subjective assumptions about the type of person who will do best in the assignment.
3. Be open to talented people who come in unfamiliar packaging.
4. Make sure you have a broad, diverse candidate pool.

Reflection

- Have you ever had the experience of hiring someone who you weren't totally comfortable with who then exceeded all of your expectations ... or hiring someone you were comfortable with who didn't work out?

CHAPTER TEN

Helping Them Win

As a manager, you might think that you have control, but you don't. You actually have less control than the people you support. Each individual employee can decide what he will do and what he will not do. He can decide how he will do it, when he will do it, and with whom he will do it. He can make things happen. As the manager, you can't make anything happen. All you can do is influence, engage, berate, cajole, and encourage, hoping that you can get most of your staff to do what you ask of them. That isn't control. That's remote control. Still, you have all the accountability for the team's performance.

To compound the problem, people are unpredictable and different. No matter how you select for certain talents, each person on your staff comes with his own style, needs, motivations, and hot buttons. This variety is the reality of diversity, and there is nothing wrong with it. In fact, having a team of people who all look at the world in slightly different ways is a real benefit, but diversity does make your job more complex. Not only do you have to manage by remote control, but you also have to take into account that each employee will respond to your signals in different ways.

Inclusion

"Managing Differently" and "inclusion" are often used synonymously. In fact, they are different but complementary concepts. Inclusion is a sense of belonging or a feeling of being a part of the group. Managing Differently helps create inclusion by demonstrating that an employee matters. Self-confidence coupled with quality effort is the basis of high performance and elevated potential. The opposite of this belief is that performance and potential are a function of innate intelligence and ability. Based on your own conditioning and value system, this belief can be the cause of exclusionary behavior toward some people or groups. Exclusion, of course, creates a self-fulfilling prophecy. If you, as a manager, have low expectations of a person, you will see low performance from that person. Remember, too, that your expectations will be difficult to fake. Employees tend to know when the manager believes in them and when the manager simply tolerates them.

In order for you to practice inclusion effectively, you must believe that every employee has enough intellectual capacity to be a peak performer. In addition, you must believe that:

- Employees can get smarter by doing and succeeding.
- Employees can control their development.
- Failure is simply feedback to inform improvement.

If you, for whatever reason, doubt that any employee can succeed, you will almost unconsciously behave toward her with condescension and low expectation. That behavior will trigger insecurity in the employee and translate into lowered performance.

Let's make this plain and simple. Can you think of any

Inclusion is a sense of belonging or a feeling of being a part of the group. *Managing Differently helps foster inclusion.*

insecurity you may have that could undermine your confidence if you were made to think about it constantly at work? For example, you may be a little self-conscious about the fact that you never completed a college degree. If others in your group are always making reference to the value of one university or another, and they all participate in informal activities that revolve around college affiliation, at an implicit level, they are conveying, "No one should be allowed to work here unless they have at least a bachelor's degree from Our Own University," and their exclusionary behavior could affect you. Now, substitute your difference into the above scene. You may be a different religion, a different ethnicity (with stereotypes attached), a different sexual orientation, or just a different personality type. Can you see how subtle exclusion could cause you to be less productive in an environment like that?

If you can in any way relate to the above situation, you should be able to appreciate the impact of exclusion and the need for inclusion. Exclusionary behavior occurs daily in almost all work places, showing up as jokes, lack of acknowledgment, designated "in" crowds, derogatory comments, treating people as "invisible," overt racism, sexist remarks, members-only informal associations, elitist assignments, and a thousand other subtle and not-so-subtle ways.

An effective diversity manager must recognize when exclusionary behaviors are occurring, take action to eliminate them, and then replace them with encouragement, support, and development for all employees.

Performance Feedback

After you have successfully learned how each employee likes to be managed, motivated, and coached (using the Managing

> You must believe that every employee has enough intellectual capacity to be a peak performer.

Differently Dialogue), you must turn to the difficult task of performance feedback. In today's environment, managers quite often go out of their way to avoid the appearance of bias, favoritism, or discrimination. In the process, they often avoid their responsibility to give effective feedback to all the people in their work group.

You may find giving feedback difficult, especially when the person you are addressing is significantly different from yourself. Feedback across differences seems to be a trap to a lot of managers. You may be fearful of retribution. You may be uncomfortable with the discomfort of the receiver, and you may be concerned that you will use inappropriate language or in some other way offend the receiver.

The key to this problem is in a deeper appreciation of the value of feedback and a repositioning of the process. Feedback must be about behavior, not about personality. Instead of positive or negative, feedback can be categorized as *adjusting* (change of behavior) or *reinforcing* (acknowledging good performance). Apprehension about differences can be addressed by simply sticking to the facts, having concrete examples, and adhering to specific, agreed-upon performance criteria. Every employee needs and deserves regular feedback. Those who get it are more likely to perform at peak levels. Those who are denied it for whatever reason are unjustly handicapped by the inadequacy of their manager.

People need just the right amount of feedback to know how well they are doing and to feel good about their manager. Lack of feedback can cause some employees to stop producing altogether. Too much feedback may make some employees nervous and promote more mistakes as the manager stands over them watching their every move. Too little feedback may allow some employees to use up all their energy and resources going in the wrong direction. Without feedback, employees are unable to objectively evaluate problems and make adjustments. Lack of feedback is tantamount to setting people up for failure.

Difficult as it may be, you have a responsibility to give feedback. Even with the discomfort of negative feedback and the uncertainty of feedback across differences, you cannot abrogate this responsibility. When employees are unsure about their performance against expectations, they assume the best. They expect the best in return. If those expectations go unmet, trouble may arise. If you fail to give timely, complete, and accurate feedback, you leave the company exposed for complaints and lawsuits.

Feedback across differences works best when the manager observes a few simple guidelines:

1. Talk about actual observations of behavior, not impressions or judgments.
2. Give specific and concrete examples.
3. Avoid inferences, judgments, or interpretations.
4. Focus on information that is likely to have value to the receiver.
5. Check to see how the receiver is responding to the information.

Remember, formal, periodic performance feedback should never be a surprise to an employee. If it is, then the feedback is being given too late.

Difficult Employees

I suspect all these principles and behaviors seem possible with most of your employees, but I also suspect that you are wondering if they will work with your difficult employee, your problem child, the chief troublemaker. Well, I want to remind you of a key concept of Managing Differently: the belief that every employee can give 100 percent and that it is the manager's responsibility to help them do it (Principle 1). So, I'm going to suggest that if you think you have a problem employee, *you may be the problem*. Also, if you think you have done all you can do to turn a problem employee into a 100 percent performer, think again. You may have only done what you know to do.

What You Need to Know

1. Effective diversity managers practice Managing Differently and make it possible for each employee to feel included.
2. Effective diversity managers practice the principles of Managing Differently as they give performance feedback.
3. If you have a difficult employee, rethink the situation. You may be part of the problem.

Reflection

- How are you currently practicing the Managing Differently principles as you coach and mentor your employees and give them feedback?
- Where do you need to be more mindful of the principles?

CHAPTER ELEVEN

Helping Them Grow

M embers of your team add value to the enterprise. Your job is to increase that value. In any organization, money, technology, equipment, and information matter. The people who work in the enterprise matter even more.

The rate at which the value of your staff increases is influenced by their natural ability (so choose well), their motivation (so give them what they need), and their opportunities to learn and grow. Developing people is about accelerating their rate of learning.

As the manager, you need to make sure that development is applied to all people on your staff, not just the "superstars." Remember, everyone has strengths. You must set out to increase the value of the collective strengths of the group.

At this point, the goal of getting 100 percent from 100 percent can be challenging—not because some employees are not willing, but because managers find it difficult to expect it from everyone. The natural tendency is to support and nurture those who match your vision of a "good" employee. The people you

> As the manager, you need to make sure that development is applied to all people on your staff, not just the "superstars."

know, like, and trust are usually the first ones in whom you will invest for development. Based on your experiences, you tend to unconsciously label employees as stars (best), average (acceptable), and duds (worst). The challenge is to find ways to make sure that everyone has an equal chance to develop and master his or her own job.

With limited resources, you may be tempted to allocate training, experiences, and your own time in ways that you feel will be most productive—that is, with the people you have deemed as worthy of development. The principles of Managing Differently suggest that you apply limited resources in a way that all employees get what they need from you.

The purpose of development activities, of course, is to accelerate the rate of learning so that employees quickly become more valuable. Development is used to better equip them for their present jobs and in some cases to prepare them for promotion or movement to other positions. The key, in either case, is to make sure each person is getting what he needs. No one should be advantaged to the disadvantage of others.

You have learned from your Managing Differently Dialogue activity that each person responds differently and each person is motivated differently. How can you use that information to get better results?

People don't change that much. No matter how you try to build a unified team with common language and common understandings of mission, each person will retain much of what makes them unique. Effective diversity managers also know that the purpose of the team is to perform. Performance means to achieve an outcome that is deemed valuable to the organization and its customers. You must accept total responsibility for focusing people toward performance, and at the same time recognize that you cannot force anyone to perform in a prescribed way.

One way to do this is to clearly define the outcomes and then let each person find her own means of achieving those outcomes. If you have been a technical star in your work, this concept could be especially difficult for you. This approach resolves the apparent dilemma of recognizing that people are different while focusing them on the same required performance. The best way to turn someone's talents into performance is to help her find her own path of least resistance toward the desired outcome.

Diversity tension is inevitable. Effective diversity managers direct that tension toward achievement by defining the right outcomes and allowing people to reach the target, not by rote mimicry of steps, but by application of their own unique creative energy.

Coaching for Results

Winston Churchill once stated that "all people love to learn, they just hate being taught." Your employees may not appreciate your efforts to teach them. For that reason, managers should think in terms of help rather than instruction. I recommend that you use language that reinforces your intent to help (e.g., "how can I help you get this done better?"). As you can see, this attitude assumes a high level of competence on the part of each employee. It acknowledges that the employee has the talent for the work, and that he has mastered the skills to perform the work. Your role (as coach) is to remind him of how good he is and what behaviors contribute to his being good. People not only love to learn, they also love and respect managers who use coaching as a helping tool.

Equal Access

In *Bringing Them In,* I discussed how unfamiliar packaging can keep you from seeing what you are looking for. But just knowing what you are looking for can be a challenge itself. It is unlikely that a manager can fully discover those characteristics and traits that she values and that are valued in the culture of the company during formal work activities. For that reason, so many organizations sponsor informal outings, and so many managers spend quality informal time with some of the employees.

It's natural that on a social basis you might prefer one employee's company over another. Be certain, however, that when the time comes to choose who will be assigned the special assignment or who will attend training, you have given each employee the opportunity to get to know you on a personal level.

Assumed Competence

I was working with a large beverage company to determine the reasons that there were so few minorities in their upper ranks. When I spoke to the minorities who had successfully made it to high positions within the company, they all told a similar story. In all cases, they were "sponsored" by respected officers in the company. This endorsement by already respected and admired individuals helped pave the way. They didn't have to spend their time and energy proving themselves. Instead, they had the confidence they needed to produce the successful results they were already capable of producing. Because they were assumed to be competent, they avoided the energy-draining process of working to be heard or overcoming invisibility. Instead they could focus on the value-added content they brought to the table.

What difference does assumed competence make? After all, people are either competent or they are not, right? Unfortunately, not so. The assumption of competence changes the dynamics of every interaction. If a person is assumed competent (by association), mistakes are tolerated and performance is expected. If a person is not assumed competent, mistakes are magnified and even great work is overlooked.

Why is it that when you walk into a meeting full of new people, you immediately judge some as competent and you reserve judgment on others? Usually the answer lies in what you have heard about them from others.

Preferential Treatment

At this point, Principle 7 becomes very important: recognizing that employees do not require the same treatment and that each should be treated differently to achieve fairness and equity. Most managers would say that preferential treatment is a bad thing. I say that when handled correctly, it can lead to effective teams and happy workers.

Preferential treatment means that everyone on your team gets special treatment, not that everyone is treated the same. As I've already described, each person has unique wants, needs, and motivations. Your job as a manager is to treat each employee as if she is your favorite employee by helping her achieve her goals. In the end, you'll be achieving your own team's goals.

An effective diversity manager understands the needs of each of her employees and is open about his management policies and principles so that all employees have clear expectations and so that jealousies do not develop. By making preferential treatment a concept that everyone on your team understands, you can avoid conflict and jealousy. Preferential treatment becomes a self-regulating option.

The key to effective preferential treatment is knowing each employee well enough to understand his or her life needs. One employee's life need may be caring for his family, while other employees may be tackling issues such as finances or care for elderly parents. Once a manager understands what personal issues may affect an employee's performance, the manager may then execute preferential treatment when necessary. The second step in the process is to effectively communicate the policy and its use with all employees.

What You Need to Know

1. Everyone has strengths.
2. Developmental activities are meant to accelerate the learning of employees so they become more valuable sooner.
3. Diversity tension is inevitable.
4. The assumption of competence produces better performance.
5. Preferential treatment is a good thing.

Reflection

- Who on your team are you least likely to see as a "superstar"?
- If you assume this person is competent, what can you do differently to help this person achieve his best?

CHAPTER TWELVE

Letting Them Go

Inevitably, even with the best hiring and management techniques employed, employees eventually move on. This workplace fact of life is one that we should celebrate instead of resist. Don't get me wrong, I'm not trying to justify people leaving because they've had a bad experience with you as a manager. People jumping ship and people moving on to better opportunities are two different things.

While most managers typically see turnover within their departments as a negative, the manager who manages differently seeks out opportunities to "turn over" her staff. If not, that means the manager is not listening to her staff and has not subscribed to the principles and tools in Part 2. One cannot expect 100 percent from her employees and subsequently not give them opportunities to advance or move on from their current roles. The fact is, your employees will move on with or without you. Why not make turnover a more positive experience?

Sometimes you need to go further than simply putting up a positive front when an employee moves on. If you are truly interested in your employee's long-term goals, you need to grease the path to help them advance. At some point, that means the employee moves on within the company and may even mean the employee must leave your company in order to pursue his goals. That's okay. It's expected. A manager who manages differently rejoices when an employee finds her next passion.

Believe it or not, turnover (if managed correctly) can have the following positive outcomes:

- Your department will gain recognition when other areas of the company benefit from your highly skilled, trained, and expertly managed staff.
- You will receive more potential applicants to open positions when word spreads from your former employees that your department is a great place to work.
- Former employees may actually return to your organization or your department if the door is left open to them and their exit was positive.

I'm sure you have heard from coworkers who complain about having their career limited by a supervisor who claims they are too valuable to let go. In cases like this, people are not submitted for new jobs and are, in fact, discouraged from self-selecting. The result is just the opposite of what the supervisor may have intended. Instead of greater productivity from a seasoned and experienced employee, they get less productivity from a disgruntled employee.

In our research, we regularly encounter employees who feel discriminated against because they are not allowed or encouraged to pursue other job opportunities. If the employees are part of a protected group, Affirmative Action category, or bargaining unit, their frustration may result in difficulty for the company. You should be very careful that you are not contributing to that kind of frustration. Think of letting them go as a natural part of the cycle of management.

Don't let turnover be a surprise. Plan for it in a positive way.

What You Need to Know

1. It's better to have people leave your group because you've prepared them for better opportunities than because they feel stifled.

Reflection

- In your career as a manager, who is the employee that you were most effective in helping to grow and then letting them go?
- What was it that made this such a positive experience?
- What can you learn from this experience that will help you develop others and push them on to other opportunities?

PART FOUR

❖ ❖ ❖

So What?

What's It All About?

The concepts, principles, and tools in this book are essential in today's workplace. They are simple. You probably already know most of them. My hope for you is that you will move past knowing them and actually develop the discipline to use them naturally and habitually. Too many recent examples are available where good people with good intentions have been assigned to jobs as managers and have done bad things unconsciously, which have caused a great deal of pain and harm to other people and to companies.

The primary (and most important) relationship at work is between employee and manager. Diversity complicates that relationship. Without the discipline to deliberately work at becoming an effective diversity manager, this important relationship provides a lot of opportunity for missteps, misconceptions, miscommunications, mistakes, and just plain misses. The stakes are high. The consequences are huge. You can no longer afford to leave it to chance. The example described in the Diversity Coach (Appendix) illustrates the kind of support you will need to develop and master the principles and tools addressed in this book. The results will show in your behavior and that of your employees.

In case you still don't see the relevance of the concepts, let me conclude by telling you what this is really all about.

It's about Dignity

I must admit that I was expecting a really cutting and vindictive exposé in the book *Roberts vs. Texaco: A True Story of Race and Corporate America*.[11] I was a part of the consulting team that worked for Texaco during the aftermath of their record-setting settlement of an employee lawsuit. I had my own impression of the company and was anxious to have Ms. Roberts tell the inside story. Instead, her story served to reinforce one of the most important lessons managers can learn about the people they serve.

Bari Ellen Roberts tells us the human side of the high-profile drama surrounding the Texaco case. She reminds us that she and all her coplaintiffs are real human beings with hopes, aspirations, needs, expectations, and commitment. She came to Texaco fully prepared and full of enthusiasm. She had unique skills that could help elevate Texaco to greater success. She relished being a part of such a highly recognized and admired company. Furthermore, she trusted her managers to recognize, respect, and use the talents she brought to the workplace. Roberts found, to her shock, that equity was not always a part of the process of managing, selecting, promoting, and honoring people.

Most managers like to demonize employees who are bodacious enough to call their company to task for not living up to their stated values. Most people assume that people who file lawsuits for discrimination or harassment are motivated by money. Bari Ellen Roberts reminds us that the key motivation is to *regain a sense of dignity.* No one really wins when employees have to sue their own company. The process is long, protracted, painful, tedious, depressing, and financially draining to the plaintiffs. The company winds up being distracted by the lawsuit and can lose momentum in key areas of the business.

Managing Differently is a way to avoid this pain. *If every manager made it her business to get to know and trust every employee, lawsuits would be unnecessary.* If every employee felt they could trust their manager and get all their concerns heard and addressed, there would be no need to take family issues outside the family.

It's about Responsibility

A vice president at a medical products company asked me to intervene in an employee relations issue involving a long-term technical employee (a black female) and a relatively new supervisor (a white male). Jim, the supervisor, was hand-selected by the vice president for an important new project involving work in a technical laboratory for a new product line. Jim inherited his staff, one who listened and complied with all of Jim's instructions and one with whom he immediately clashed.

Audrey was a long-term employee who knew almost everyone in the company, including the president. Her last assignment was in a traditional laboratory function where innovation and creativity were rewarded and encouraged. However, Jim always insisted that everything be done one way: his way. After months of what seemed to be culture clash, she became frustrated with Jim. She began to complain, but all her complaints seemed to fall on deaf ears. Audrey escalated her case to her supervisor's management and eventually all the way to the president. At the point I entered the situation, Audrey had filed an Equal Employment Opportunity Commission (EEOC) complaint complete with legal representation.

After some investigation and discussion with all the parties involved, I found that the problem was simply one of different communication styles, unclear expectations, and a lack of attention to relationship building. I placed most of the responsibility on the manager. When I presented my findings and recommendations to the vice president, he blew a fuse. He said, "I can't support this report. This is not what I expected." When I asked him why he didn't support it, he stated, "I always believe my managers over an employee." With that comment, the source of the problem became even more clear.

The vice president had hired Jim because of his vast experience in a regulated lab environment. His only stated expectation was that Jim get approval of the new product line. Instead, Jim should have been told that not only was he responsible for getting results, but that he was also responsible for getting those results by creating an effective work environment and by creating effective relationships.

This case also illustrates several challenges that come with diversity and management. Audrey, and to some extent Jim, felt that the problems they were experiencing were racial. After all, he's a white male and new to the company. She is a black female and an old-timer. Quite often in cases of conflict between people, *race and gender are blamed for things that have nothing to do with race and gender.* Second, many observers would suggest that both parties contributed to the conflict. While this is true, the responsibility cannot be shared equally. The manager, simply because he is the manager, bears a greater part of the responsibility for ineffective relationships and lapses in performance (Principle 2).

Managing Differently clearly requires managers to accept their responsibility and accountability for building relationships that achieve results.

It's about Trust

One of the most difficult challenges you have as a manager is earning the trust of all your employees. To trust you means they believe in your honesty, integrity, and positive intentions toward them. When they trust you, they are willing to be vulnerable with you in situations where they cannot necessarily

> Race and gender get blamed for things that have nothing to do with race and gender.

predict the outcome. They trust that you will not take advantage of them. They feel cared about and respected.

Trust is essential to high-performing teams. Some obvious behaviors—such as criticism, judgment, superiority, and indifference—undermine trust. You can control these behaviors. You have less control over some other things that undermine trust: stereotypes, biases, prejudices, preconceptions, assumptions, and preferences. If you are not aware of these silent barriers to trust, you face a tough time winning the trust of all your employees.

So, let me encourage you again. You can master these skills and become a valuable asset to your company by *learning to be an effective diversity manager, adapting to the unique needs of each employee, and managing your own preferences, biases, stereotypes, and reactions. I call this* Managing Differently.

What You Need to Know

1. You can become an effective diversity manager and a more valuable asset for your company.
2. People crave and deserve dignity at work.
3. You have a responsibility to build relationships that get results.
4. Trust is essential to high-performing teams.

Reflection

- Are you qualified to be a manager of people?
- Do you genuinely care that people have a good experience at work?
- Are you trustworthy? What would your employees say?

The Diversity Coach™

Making the transition to become an effective diversity manager cannot be done without some support and deliberate development for several reasons:

- Old habits die hard.
- It's not natural to appreciate differences.
- We all tend to defend the rightness of what we are currently doing.

You need help—someone to listen to your plans, to question you, to direct you, and to encourage your development as an effective diversity manager. We recommend two options: peer allies and The Diversity Coach.™ A coach is someone who reminds you what you already know to do but are not doing. A coach also helps to accelerate your growth and learning.

The following example illustrates how The Diversity Coach™ can help move you past your blind spots, give you a different perspective, and help give you some accountability for your growth and development.

Coaches' Corner

Marty the Manager knew he was scheduled for a round of interviews to fill the new position. He wanted to make sure he chose well because this person would probably be a key member of the planning team for some time. The coach had reminded him that he must always begin by identifying specifically what the job requirements are and what he was looking for in a candidate, not only in terms of technical skills and abilities but the other characteristics and traits that would allow the person to fit and be successful with his team.

So, Marty sat down and reflected on those things that he and the company expected from associates. He also considered the attributes that had made others on the team successful. Finally, he thought about his own personal work-style preferences. What traits would make it likely that he would support this person toward success?

The list looked like this:

We Expect	Successful Associates Always Have	I Like
Loyalty	Sense of Humor	Intelligence
Honesty	Ability to Focus	Respectfulness
Integrity	Commitment to Job	Enthusiasm

Marty was feeling pretty good with this list. He thought, *What a sophisticated and honest way to make a decision. My diversity coach was right; this approach makes sense.*

Just as he was about to stand up and go to the conference room to prepare for the first interview, he heard the whistle and the coach appeared again. Before the coach could say anything, Marty blurted out quickly, "I'm glad you're here. You will be proud. Look at this list of requirements. And I'm going to use targeted selection procedures to make sure I ask the right questions. I know what I am looking for."

The coach gave the time-out sign and said, "Sure, you know what you are looking for, but, how will you know it when you see it?"

Marty said, "What do you mean?"

The coach began, "Marty, look carefully at your list. Now close your eyes. Based on that list, try to visualize the perfect candidate. Think deep. And when you have the picture in your mind, tell me what you see."

Marty thought and thought. Then he said, "Okay, I see *him*."

The coach said, "Describe *him* to me."

Marty did so. It included his being tall, white, neatly cut dark hair, slim, dressed in a blue suit, carrying a personal organizer, and a degree from WOW U. The coach said, "Why do you think *he* looks like that?"

Marty said, "I don't know."

The coach said, "It's because that is the package you most associate with the traits you are looking for in a candidate. And if you are honest, you will see that the package is very much like yourself. It is also like those people who have been your best employees in the past."

Marty asked, "Well, is that wrong?"

The coach said, "Not necessarily, but remember the criteria you established in your list. That is what you are really looking for, and it is the right stuff. The problem is you may only be able to see it when it comes in a familiar package. Could you recognize it in an unfamiliar package?

"It is also possible," the coach continued, "that you are unconsciously perpetuating your own kind. Your own kind does not necessarily mean your race-gender mix, but people who share your background, your training, your preferences, and other dimensions of diversity that you happen to know, like, and trust."

Marty thought about it, and he remembered that the last three employees he had hired were all from the state university, they all had engineering degrees, they all grew up in the Midwest, and they all seemed to him to be deep thinkers.

Marty asked the coach, "How will I know if I am selecting based on my preferences, comfort, or stereotypes?"

The coach responded, "Let us think about that together. If you have been selecting from a diverse pool of candidates (big net) and you consistently choose a single profile, it would be a clue that your comfort, preferences, and stereotypes are affecting your decision. It does not mean you have made the wrong choices; it merely raises the question. Is it logical and reasonable to expect that only those who match your subconscious profile are good candidates for your team?"

The coach went on to say, "It is important that the individual you select be a good fit. You are more likely to help them succeed if you feel that they fit in. But, you must be sure that you are fishing with a big net (getting the best from all available pools), that you recognize the power of your subjective criteria, and that you are willing to risk selecting someone who may be packaged differently."

• • • •

The Diversity Coach™ is a registered trademark of J.O. Rodgers and Associates, Inc. Management Consultants.

Managers who want to accelerate their development can get advice and suggestions about specific Diversity Management challenges by logging on to *www.thediversitycoach.com* and accessing The Diversity Coach™ option. You may also mail questions to:

> The Diversity Coach™
> c/o J.O. Rodgers and Associates, Inc.
> 3951 Snapfinger Parkway
> Suite 440
> Decatur, Georgia 30035

Endnotes

[1] Certified Management Consultant, a designation granted by the Institute of Management Consultants (IMC), which represents the highest standards of consulting and adherence to the ethical canons of the profession. Fewer than 1 percent of all consultants have achieved this level of performance.

[2] Marcus Buckingham and Curt Coffman, *First, Break All the Rules: What the World's Greatest Managers Do Differently* (New York: Simon and Schuster, 1999).

[3] Terrence Deal and Allan Kennedy Deal, *The New Corporate Cultures: Revitalizing the Workplace after Downsizing, Mergers, and Reengineering.* (Reading, MA: Perseus Books, 1999). John Kotter and James Heskett, *Corporate Culture and Performance* (New York: The Free Press, 1992).

[4] Peter F. Drucker, *Management Challenges for the 21st Century* (New York: HarperCollins, 1999).

[5] "Managing Diversity" was coined to emphasize the importance of creating organizational environments that were inclusive and which fully tapped into the potential of a diverse workforce.

[6] The definition of "Managing Differently" is learning to be an effective manager of people and then adapting to the unique needs of each individual while managing your own preferences, biases, stereotypes, and reactions.

[7] R. Roosevelt Thomas Jr., *Redefining Diversity* (New York: AMACOM, 1996), 83–84.

[8] In actuality the only group not covered are able-bodied white men under forty who are not Vietnam veterans.

[9] Drucker, *Management Challenges in the 21st Century.*

[10] The Belief System™ is a registered trademark of Dr. Thad Green. For more information on The Belief System Concepts, read Dr. Green's book entitled *The Belief System of Motivation and Performance.*

[11] Bari Ellen Roberts, *Roberts vs. Texaco: A True Story of Race and Corporate America* (New York: Avon Books, 1999).

I N D E X

Jim Rodgers, CMC is in the performance business. He has been a confidential change agent for dozens of leaders at some of America's "Best" companies. Jim has developed a unique approach to managing the complexity in the workplace. He has published over 20 articles, delivered over 50 speeches, and has become the leading advocate for using the principles of diversity management and inclusion as a strategy to manage complexity, achieve specific objectives, and to improve overall performance. His clients have come to appreciate his uncommon wisdom, his mastery at facilitating courageous conversations, and his natural ability to coach and advise senior leaders.

Jim is a Certified Management Consultant (CMC), which represents the highest standards in consulting and adherence to the ethical canons of the profession. Less than 1% of all management consultants have achieved this level of performance.

Please contact Jim to learn more about his work:

J.O. Rodgers & Associates, Inc.

3951 Snapfinger Parkway, Suite 440, Decatur, Georgia, 30035

Phone: 404-286-1234 • Fax: 404-286-2336,

Email: jor@managingdifferently.com

www.managingdifferently.com

www.thediversitycoach.com